The Working Musician's Handbook for Professional Success

The Working Musician's Handbook for Professional Success

How to Establish Your Value in the Real World

Kris Hawkins

Rowman & Littlefield
Lanham • Boulder • New York • London

Published by Rowman & Littlefield
An imprint of The Rowman & Littlefield Publishing Group, Inc.
4501 Forbes Boulevard, Suite 200, Lanham, Maryland 20706
www.rowman.com

86-90 Paul Street, London EC2A 4NE

Edited by Ronny S. Schiff
Additional Credits: Portrait photographs by Littil Swayamp

British Library Cataloguing in Publication Information Available

Library of Congress Cataloging-in-Publication Data

Names: Hawkins, Kris, 1979– author.
Title: The working musician's handbook for professional success : how to establish your value in the real world / Kris Hawkins.
Description: Lanham : Rowman & Littlefield, 2022. | Series: Music pro guides | Includes bibliographical references and index. | Summary: "A no-nonsense handbook on how to establish value as a professional musician and create a sustainable career in the working world, written by an EMMY-award winning, veteran practitioner"— Provided by publisher.
Identifiers: LCCN 2021057487 (print) | LCCN 2021057488 (ebook) | ISBN 9781538161982 (cloth) | ISBN 9781538161999 (paperback) | ISBN 9781538162002 (epub)
Subjects: LCSH: Music trade—Vocational guidance.
Classification: LCC ML3795 .H38 2022 (print) | LCC ML3795 (ebook) | DDC 780.23—dc23
LC record available at https://lccn.loc.gov/2021057487
LC ebook record available at https://lccn.loc.gov/2021057488

For my mother, Rebecca.
You never stopped believing in me, you never stopped pushing me,
and you never gave up on me.
You are the strongest person I know.

CONTENTS

CONTENTS

CONTENTS

LIST OF FIGURES

LIST OF FIGURES

ACKNOWLEDGMENTS

There are so many I wish to thank for making this book a reality. I guess the best place to begin is at the beginning.

This whole journey began with Joe Braccio. Joe built the musical foundations upon which the entirety of my career sits. Without his guidance, wisdom, and encouragement, I wouldn't be who I am today.

Kenny Walker. Dr. LoHertz himself. Kenny showed me how to not just play the music but how to "feel" it.

Anthony "Brew" Brewster. When I was about to give up and leave Los Angeles with my tail between my legs, Brew gave me a musical "home" in which to reside. Almost two decades later, I'm still here and forever grateful for his guidance in both life and music.

Pete Antunes. For your steadfast friendship and fierce loyalty through thick and thin. Pete is my brother from another mother.

The House of Vibe All-Stars. Deploi, Phil D. Fish, C. Wolfe, Ray Ray, Amy Lou, SeaBass, Bill, Ric'key, Desi, and all the amazing musicians that would come through on a Wednesday night in Santa Monica. They consistently raised the bar of what I was capable of. (Plus, for letting me play an extended version of "Maggot Brain" every week.)

ACKNOWLEDGMENTS

Mikal Reid. A great mentor and an even better friend. Mikal lifted me up when I was at my lowest and asked for nothing in return. His selflessness and caring for those around him are unmatched by any other.

Tyler Conti. My musical compatriot and greatest collaborator. Tyler always urges me to see my potential. I look forward to continuing this journey we've been on.

Francis Buckley. A man whose insight, wisdom, and hilarious stories have enlightened me and reminded me that there is always humor to be found among the absurd.

Littl Swayamp. For making me look presentable with your fabulous photographs.

The staff and faculty at the Musicians Institute College of Contemporary Music, most notably Jonathan Newkirk and Krystal Schafer. Jonathan, for allowing me the freedom to teach in my own "unique" way. And for being a boss "boss." Krystal, for the fact that nothing would ever get done if it weren't for her. You are the Svengali of making things happen, and you are appreciated.

All of my students, past, present, and future. For pushing me to stay current and for calling me on my bullshit when necessary. You keep me humble.

Ronny Schiff. For believing that I had something to say and helping me find my voice to say it. Not only is she a fantastic editor, but she has also become one of my nearest and dearest friends.

Michael Tan at Rowman & Littlefield Publishing Group for taking a chance with me and believing in the subject matter of this book.

Rose[2]. For always showing up when I've needed you most. I'll never be able to express in words what it means to me. So I'll just say this: "Very basketball."

INTRODUCTION

When I first moved to Los Angeles, I had the same ambitious ideas about what I was going to do, just as the thousands of other people that move there every day. I purged anything that wasn't necessary, loaded up my truck with only my gear and my clothes, and headed west to see what I could accomplish.

I was very fortunate that within six months of my arrival, I was working as a session musician for one of the biggest music producers of the day. I thought that I had made it. I was working in a million-dollar studio every day. Famous artists, writers, and managers were coming through all the time. I was playing guitar on tons of tracks. I wasn't making great money, but I thought to myself, "Hey, just being around all this, something has got to break. Right?"

Not so much.

I realized rather quickly how grossly underequipped I was for dealing with the industry at that level. I was okay in the technical sense; I had studied music formally in both high school and college. I knew all my scales and chords; I could play almost anything anyone would ask of me. My shortfall was having no understanding of things like publishing, PROs, royalties, and, especially, a general sense of how the music business *actually* operated, or how one would make a living working within it.

In the end, my lack of understanding of the business aspects was taken advantage of. For four years I worked fifteen hours a day, seven days a week, making a pittance every week, and just churned out ideas for these people. Being the only "musician" in the room—meaning the only person who knew how to actually play an instrument—made me a valuable commodity to these people. And they took full advantage. What I didn't understand was that I was "writing and creating" and, therefore, was entitled to the credits and ownership that came along with these undertakings. Whenever I asked how this all worked, I was told, "Don't worry, we'll take care of you." Oh, they took care of me all right—they took all my writer's credits and publishing.

The realization dawned that I was being used for my abilities with no intention of real compensation for my efforts. So after four years, I had no other choice than to walk away with nothing.

It felt like starting over again. I had been in Los Angeles for almost five years, and because I spent all my time holed up in a studio, I had to create a whole new network of people in order to get working again.

Over the course of the next few years, I dedicated my time to learning as much as I could about the business side of the music industry. To fill in the "gaps" that my formal music education never covered.

What didn't occur to me initially was that I was not alone in my struggles. That there were countless musicians out there that had the same gaps in their musical "business" knowledge as well.

This book is the culmination of my experiences navigating the precarious waters of the industry, ultimately arriving at the safe shoreline of a lasting and sustainable career as a musician. Additionally, this is information that I have shared with hundreds of students over the past decade with gratifying results.

I'm not going to promise you great success or riches beyond belief if you read this book. The amount of success you have will be directly related to your drive and determination to succeed.

What I can promise is that this book will help set the stage for your success. By the end, you'll have a grasp on:

- How to assert your value as a musician

- How to find gigs and what to charge for your services

- How to protect your work

- What Performing Rights Organizations are and how royalties work

- How to work for yourself

- How to deal with the inevitable setbacks you will face and how to overcome them

Plus, you'll find checklists that will keep you organized for various situations, such as:

- Touring Checklist

- Live Playing Checklist

- Studio Checklist for Engineers

- Studio Checklist for Producers

- Studio Checklist for Session Musicians

- Media Composer Checklist

- Teaching Checklist

Your path may differ greatly from mine, and you are sure to face perilous waters of your own. So although I won't profess to have all the answers, I can offer my own experiences and insights from over two decades in the industry. My hope is that this book will help you learn from my mistakes and avoid some of the major pitfalls that I fell into. You'll have your own setbacks, but armed with some knowledge, you'll be able to recover and learn from them much faster.

Kris Hawkins

The amount of success you have will be directly related to your drive and determination to succeed.

ESTABLISHING YOUR VALUE AS A MUSICIAN

CSA Images/Getty Images

So you've made the conscious decision to take your music career a step further. As Obi Wan Kenobi says, "You've taken your first step into a larger world." This is also the point at which the fear and the self-doubt begin to take hold. You may have some people in your life that will question your decision. That's okay. This path isn't for everyone. You will have to overcome many obstacles, the greatest of them being you, yourself. But fear not. While difficult, it is not impossible. To help you along your journey, here is one rule that you should have etched into your mind:

Never Do Anything for Free (Unless You Want To)

Read this, then read it again. Burn it into your subconscious so every decision, henceforth, is held up against it.

The Rapid Devaluation of the Music Industry

The reason many will not succeed in this business is because they never learn to value fully what it is that they do. While any venture in the arts is a noble endeavor, society tends to look down upon the artist.

Music, especially, has been severely devalued over the last few decades. Beginning with the advent of Napster in the 1990s, iTunes, and finally with streaming services of today. It used to be that if you wanted to listen to a particular song, you had to go to a record store and pay sometimes upward of $16 for an album just to get a copy of the one song you wanted for your own enjoyment. Nowadays, for better or for worse, you have access to any type of music whenever and wherever you want.

Because there is no cost or risk associated with listening to your favorite song, people just assume that they are entitled to it and, therefore, the artist should just be grateful someone is listening at all.

Beyoncé or Broke

In the eyes of those outside the music industry, if you're not on TV or in the media every day, you must not be very good at what you do and are probably incapable of generating any income with your art. If you're not Beyoncé, you must be broke.

What the average listener fails to realize is that between these two extremes, there is a world of opportunities for a musician to make a real and decent living pursuing their passion. There are producers, songwriters, film composers, engineers, session musicians, studio operators, software developers, teachers, and more. Each of these paths is a necessary and viable link in the chain of the industry.

> Between these two extremes, there is a world of opportunities for a musician to make a real and decent living pursuing their passion.

It may take a while for you to find your path within the business, but I assure you that once you do find it, there is nothing (save for yourself) that can stop you from achieving whatever it is that you desire.

Experience and Exposure

You pick up your first instrument, write your first song, or create your first beats because you find that it's something that makes you happy. You're not thinking about money or a career. You do it because something resonates within you.

As you progress in your craft, you begin to daydream about what it would be like making this thing that brings you so much joy, your career. This is the point at which those voices in your head start to chime in and say, "It's not safe" or "You're not good enough."

You have to make a conscious decision that *this is for you*. This is the path that you're going to take. Once you've decided this, now begins the effort to turn this passion into a sustainable career.

The problem many face at this point is that most don't have the first idea about how to begin making money with their talent.

"When I began my career as a professional, I remember I almost felt guilty accepting any form of compensation for the gigs that I was doing. I was just happy to be on a stage. It was everything I had ever wanted, and I was getting paid to do it. I felt validated in my decision to become a professional. As time went on, I would do any gig for any amount of money, or even no money at all. I was just happy to be asked to do something."

This mindset is where many will get into trouble in the beginning. You're so happy to do anything at all that involves your passion, that you feel almost ashamed to assume that you could be compensated for it. There are those in the world that understand this about creative types and will try to use this to exploit you. Terms like "experience" and "exposure" get thrown around a lot.

"Hey man! You should totally play this show; there's no money, but it will be great exposure for your band!"

or

"I've got this song I need recorded, I don't have any cash, but you need the experience because you're just starting out."

Yes, you do need both "experience" and "exposure" to progress in your career. However, you should always remember to get them on your own terms, not anyone else's. You will be the one who decides if an opportunity is the right opportunity for you or not.

Understand that there are those that will try to guilt you into doing things for these reasons. They will use your passion and love for your craft against you. At the end of the day, the decision lies wholly with you.

Establishing Your Value

"When talking to my students about establishing their value, the easiest method that I came up with to get them to start looking at what they do as a valuable asset was this: I would simply ask them how much time and money they were spending to learn the things they were learning.

"I would then ask them if they were spending all this time and money to go out and just give away all the skills and knowledge they have acquired."

Most got the point right away.

When you take your personal time and personal money to further your knowledge of your chosen craft, you need to consider it as an investment. And like any good investment, you expect it will bring a decent return.

Would you expect a doctor or a lawyer, who spends an enormous amount of time learning their trade, to just graduate and start working for free? Sounds ridiculous. Because it is ridiculous.

There is no difference between a doctor, a plumber, a computer programmer, or a professional musician. They are all skilled positions that require an investment of time and money by the individual to master. Only, the musician isn't always taken seriously. So you have to be the one to take yourself seriously and convey that to others.

You may not have gone to a school that specializes in music, and that's okay. You don't need school to establish your value. *What you do need is a commitment to your craft.* Take stock in how much time you spend learning new things, investing in equipment, taking lessons. Begin to consider all of these things as an investment. The more you invest, you more value you build.

Here's an easy way to begin to understand this concept. Next time someone asks you to play a gig, work on a track, or anything that involves your craft. Ask yourself this question: "Why are they asking me to do this?"

The answer is an easy one. They are asking you because they don't have the ability to do it themselves. They haven't invested either the time or money to learn how to do what you can do—you have. In this moment, you should realize that you have the upper hand. You have something that they want or need. You are valuable to them. Understanding this concept is the first step in establishing your value.

Education

In order to be successful, you need to bring something to the table. This means you will have to spend a considerable amount of time educating yourself within your chosen path. While technology affords you the ability to look up and learn almost anything these days on your own, you will have to invest your time and some of your money possibly to further your ambitions.

Learning on Your Own

Fortunately, you live in a world where almost all the knowledge that you could ever desire is accessible with the touch of a button. Never before have you had so many options to learn about whatever you can imagine. There are entire YouTube channels devoted to particular skillsets and instruments. There are online courses that have high-quality tutorials and instructional videos.

With a little digging, you can find whatever it is that you're looking for. Just be aware that not all the information out there is always correct. Take everything with a grain of salt. Remember, when it comes to being creative with your musical skillset, there are no rules, only guidelines, so be wary of those that say that this is the "only" way. Other than that, take whatever you can from the resources available.

Private Lessons

Studying with someone who is currently doing the things that you want to do is an excellent way of furthering your education. It's important to find the right teacher for whatever your goals are. Do some research in your local area; find out about whom everyone is talking. There are always a few names that will rise to the top. Go with those.

Private lessons can get expensive. So if you can't afford a full month of lessons, see if you can work something out with the instructor where you come in once a month and receive a shot of information.

College and Trade Schools

This obviously will be the most expensive educational option. However, you get what you pay for. Another option: your local region may have a junior college that offers classes in the area in which you are interested. You can take one or two classes to see if it's a good fit. The quality of the teachers is usually higher than most other situations. If you are able, this may be a good option.

Internships

If you know someone in your area that runs a studio or performs around town frequently, you could ask them if they would be interested in having someone help them out with various tasks in exchange for their wisdom.

You may have to get coffee or pick up dry cleaning; you may become like a personal assistant to them. However, in exchange for helping them out, they may share their insights and experiences with you.

An internship could even lead to your first real gig.

Always remember that with internships, you are choosing to be there. If you feel that you aren't gaining any knowledge or experience from it, you can always walk away and find another.

One Percent Better

The most important thing to understand about educating yourself is this—you will never learn everything. But equally important is never becoming stagnate. It may seem overwhelming at times to learn new things. With any art form, you must be willing to commit to continuous exploration of new ideas and technologies. This is the only way to assure that you will establish the resources necessary to become a master at your craft.

Dedicate yourself to spending time every day to work on your craft, to learn one new thing—just one. Discipline yourself to get one percent better. Develop this into a habit. While slow at first, with dedication and time, you will begin to reap the benefits of exponentially increasing your knowledge and understanding in your chosen field.

Plus, doing this will increase your self-confidence and the confidence you have in your abilities. You will begin to feel and understand that the knowledge you possess is valuable.

Balance

The first part of this chapter has been devoted to the idea that what you do is valuable and why you should "Never do anything for free." One thing that hasn't been discussed, though, is *balance*.

Like any other profession, music as a career can turn into a grind. If all you ever do is treat it like a job, then like any other job, you can quickly burn out.

You must strike a balance between the work you do for money and the things you do just for the love of it.

Never forget why you started in the first place. This is the "unless you want to" part of the rule.

If a gig comes along and they have no way of compensating you, but you love the music and the people involved—*do it*. Always remember to reignite the passion that got you going in the first place. However, also remember that the decision is yours to make, and no one else's.

One Final Thought on Education

Don't forget to educate yourself in things other than your chosen craft. It's fine to be obsessed with gaining as much knowledge about your industry as possible, but equally important is to learn about the world around you. Read a book on something you know nothing about. Take a cooking class. Experience life. Great art comes from life experiences—lost loves, failed endeavors, and, conversely, all the beautiful things in the world. Art is a representation of life; with no life—no art.

FINDING YOUR PATH

Diverstudio/Getty Images

"*In my late twenties, I ended up in what would be considered a less than ideal situation. After working professionally for nearly a decade, I found myself with no money and no place to live. I was essentially broke and homeless. I had become the stereotypical musician who couldn't keep his sh*t together.*

"*Fortunately, I had friends with couches, so I never ended up on the street or having to live out of my truck. But the feeling of being a total and complete failure was real.*

"*To make matters worse, this all happened right around the holidays, so it was extra depressing. I had a lot of time to sit and think about the situation that I had landed in and began to try and piece together where things went wrong.*

"*The thing that bothered me the most was that if I had sat down and written out all of my accomplishments up to that point—all of the big records, the artists, the tours, shows, students, etc.—at least on paper, I would have appeared to be an extremely successful musician. Yet, there I was spending the holidays on a friend's futon with nowhere else to go.*

"*It wasn't until my mom sent me a book that Christmas that I began to understand what had really happened.*

"*It was a book about setting goals. And how we have to be careful that we set the 'right' goals for ourselves.*

"So as I read through it, everything started making sense as to how I ended up here. I had set the wrong goal for myself. Now the question was when did I do this and how can I fix it? I traced it all the way back to when I was a teenager and a conversation that I had with my mother over my most recent report card.

"My mom had burst into my room as I was practicing, angrily waving my report card and asking me something to the extent of 'What are you going to do with your life?' And clear as day, I remembered the answer I gave her. I said 'Mom, I'll be happy if I can survive *doing music the rest of my life.' Boom! There it was. It hit me like a truck. I had spent the entirety of my professional career with the mindset of just 'surviving.' And that's exactly what I was doing, 'surviving.' Not thriving, not being financially stable, not being successful. I was exactly where I 'wanted' to be, or at least I told myself that up to this point in my life.*

"A change was needed, and a drastic one, fast."

And that's exactly what I was doing, "surviving."
Not thriving.

Goals

Setting goals is something that generally everyone seems to understand as a good idea. However, most end up doing it incorrectly. A goal is necessary with any endeavor. A goal provides direction, a road map of sorts, so you can navigate the turbulent waters of whatever it is you want out of your life. But understanding how to set the "right" goals for yourself is the difference between success and failure.

The first step in setting a goal is to figure out what it is that you want. This may seem easy at first, but it requires a lot of soul searching to really home in on an answer. You may say to yourself, "I want to be a professional singer." That's a start, but then what? You could end up being a professional singer that plays dive bars for the entirety of your career. Is that what you meant?

Words

When you set a goal for yourself, you need to be absolutely aware of the words you are using to describe what you want. The saying "Careful what you wish for because you just might get it" applies here.

You have to be specific and precise with the words you use to describe what you want. So you may say to yourself, *"I want to be a professional singer, releasing new music every year, touring small theatres, and making a minimum of $100,000 a year."*

That's better. Now, you have some clear-cut things for which you are aiming.

"For me, this was the game changer. Up to that point, I had spent my entire career with the mindset of just surviving. And that's exactly what I did to the letter. So once I understood this idea, I changed my goal of surviving to wanting to earn a very specific dollar amount. I had never done that before. I had never assigned a monetary value to my career. I used to do every gig that came along because it always lined up with my 'survival' mentality. I never really questioned how much I would be paid or if I would be credited properly. I was just happy with 'surviving.'

"When I shifted to my new monetary goal, something extraordinary happened. Those same gigs that I had done for years for free or for very little money no longer fit with my new direction. I began holding every opportunity up against this new goal, and if it didn't line up and move me closer to where I wanted to go, I wouldn't do it. It was almost as if subconsciously I began saying no to things. Also, up to this point, I had never in my career turned down a gig.

"At first, it felt wrong to turn down these opportunities, especially when I was in the situation that I was in. However, I knew deep down that it was the right thing to do. Continuing to do things the same way I had been wouldn't have led me out of my dilemma.

"I angered a lot of people that I had worked with up to that point. They couldn't understand why, all of a sudden, I was demanding that I be compensated properly for my time. I ended up losing about 90 percent of my gigs. But here's the part where things start to turn around. With the few gigs that did remain, when I demanded to be taken care of properly, they obliged. They understood the value that I brought to the table. One client even asked me one time, what had taken me so long to start demanding more money. He knew all along I was worth it. I just never asked."

When you get specific with your goals, you are able to make better decisions when opportunity is presented. Having a clearly defined idea of what you want makes the choices you make about where and when to spend your time much easier. You will learn to see the things that are beneficial and act on them, while avoiding the things that will waste your precious time.

Go Big or Go Home

There is absolutely no reason whatsoever to be shy when setting a goal for yourself. In fact, the bigger the better. If it sounds completely insane to you right now, then you're probably on the right track.

Small goals are easy. We achieve them every single day; there's no risk with a small goal. Therefore, the rewards if any are negligible. This is where most people end up: they fulfill the small goals of everyday life; they've chosen a "safe" career because it checks some of the small-goal boxes.

If you really want to make a go at being a professional musician, you need to think bigger, much bigger.

Here's an example:

"You want to be a professional singer and win a Grammy within the next two years."

Win a Grammy? You haven't even started your professional career yet! The physical Grammy is not the point. The idea of what it takes to win one, is.

You've probably heard the saying "Shoot for the moon." There is a second part to this that goes "Even if you miss, you'll land among the stars."

A small goal will yield small results. A big one, however, can launch you into places you never dared dream before.

Crazy as it sounds, if you set a Grammy as a goal, what will happen is you will begin to make decisions based on whether what you are doing is Grammy worthy or not. After two years of this mindset, you may not win the actual award, but one thing is assured—you will have raised the quality of you and your work to be in the orbit of those who have won them.

Set a Deadline

You must give yourself a deadline to achieve your goals. Without one, it will never seem like an urgent matter. This will help motivate you every day to move closer to what you want. Make sure that your deadline is reasonable. Larger goals may take a year or more to achieve, while smaller ones may need only a few months.

Get into the habit of when you wake up every day, ask yourself this question: *"What am I going to do today to get closer to* [insert goal here]*?"*

This is important, especially when you first wake up and your mind is clear. This will get your ideas flowing. It will help open your eyes to new opportunities. Some that may have been staring you in the face this entire time, you just didn't have a clear enough mind to see yet.

Then, as you go to bed at the end of the day, ask yourself another question: *"What did I do today to get closer to* [insert goal here]*?"*

This is more important than the morning question. This is how you will hold yourself accountable. When you answer this question, it is imperative that you are honest with yourself. If you slacked off all day and did nothing to progress, you will need to own that. So hold yourself responsible for your actions or lack thereof.

Goals can be magical things, but they do not work without action. If you sit around with a goal in mind but do nothing to move toward it, then you are just wishing. A wish is a goal with no energy; it's useless.

Only you are responsible for making your goals become a reality. No one can do this for you. Your success or failure is entirely up to you. And if you are dishonest with yourself, nothing will ever change.

Write It Down

One of the most important yet overlooked steps in the goal-setting process is writing it down. This means pen to paper. While you can put these things on your phone or computer, there is a magic in physically writing what you want out of your life on a piece of paper. It makes it real. It now exists in the universe as a tangible thing. You can look at it. Touch it. Hold it.

This is also important because when you wake up every morning, as you are asking yourself what you are going to do today, you can look at your goals. Reread them again and again. Burn them into your subconscious. Do the same thing as you go to bed every night. Make them the first thing you see when you wake up and the last thing you see when you go to bed.

GOAL WORKSHEET

What do I want? (Be specific.)

_____

_____

_____

_____

_____

When do I want it?

_____

_____

_____

_____

What am I going to do (starting right now) to get there?

_____

_____

_____

_____

What did I do today to move closer to my goal?

_____

_____

_____

_____

Figure 2.1. Goal Worksheet
Author

Creating a Mind Storm

One of the more difficult things about setting a (BIG) goal for yourself will be the fact that you have absolutely no idea where to start once you've set it.

You need to create a *mind storm*.

This is a brainstorming technique used often in business training that can help set a clear path to achieving what you want.

- The first step is to have a clearly defined goal, with a deadline.

- Next, you will need a sheet of paper and a pen.

- Now, with your goal in mind. Write out twenty different ways of achieving it.

- For example, use the goal of

  "Become a professional singer and win a Grammy within the next two years."

Now, write down everything you can think of that you will need to do to make this goal a reality. It could go something like this:

1. Get better at writing songs

2. Take more vocal lessons

3. Write better lyrics

4. Book more shows

5. Etc.

Continue doing this until you reach twenty things that you can do to move closer to your goal.

This may seem like an easy exercise, but the further down the list you go, the more difficult it is to come up with new ideas. However, that's the point of this—to get your mind churning and working on things you can do right now to start moving forward. This exercise can also help define a clear path for you so that you know on what you should be focusing your time and energy.

Setting a goal is the first step in achieving success. It will give you a direction and a purpose. You must make sure that you set the "right" goal for yourself. Be specific. Go big. Set a deadline. And mind storm it.

You may find that when you set off on your path, you may discover a new direction that you want to take that deviates from the initial plan. That's okay. You'll realize that as you progress with anything, there may be a new way of doing something, or you'll see an opportunity that you hadn't thought of before. Bend with the wind. As long as you're moving forward, you're doing it right. It's only when you stop or move in reverse that you have to worry.

MIND STORM WORKSHEET

What is my goal?

List twenty ways to achieve it.

1.) _____

2.) _____

3.) _____

4.) _____

5.) _____

6.) _____

7.) _____

8.) _____

9.) _____

10.) _____

11.) _____

12.) _____

13.) _____

14.) _____

15.) _____

16.) _____

17.) _____

18.) _____

19.) _____

20.) _____

Figure 2.2. Mind Storm Worksheet
Author

CHAPTER THREE
FINDING WORK AND NETWORKING

bsd555/Getty Images

S o you've put some thought into what you want out of your career by establishing some goals. Plus, you've started to get into the mindset that what you do is valuable. Now, you need to start applying them to finding work within your skillset to support your journey in achieving these goals.

Establishing Your Skills

Before you start searching for opportunities, you should first assess your skills:

- What are you good at?

- Is there anything special that sets you apart from others doing the same thing?

- And most importantly, who requires the services that you can provide?

It may help you to sit down with a piece of paper and write out all the things you're capable of doing. Make a detailed list. And from that list, try to see all the different avenues that you could exploit using those skills. For instance, are you good at running a digital audio workstation (DAW) like Pro Tools? Aside from the obvious of using this skill to record, edit, and mix for clients, perhaps you could also train someone who just bought their first system and has no idea how to use it.

There's a saying that goes like this:

"From one thing, know ten thousand things."

—Miyamoto Musashi, *The Book of Five Rings*, 1645 CE

What this proverb is saying is that you should look at all of the different avenues you could pursue just using one of the skills you already possess. Then do the same for any other skills you possess. And before you know it, you'll see an entire world of possibilities that you may not have seen before, all using things you already know how to do.

This is a great way to find alternate paths to creating a supplemental income stream to finance the things you really want to do.

Core Skills

Before moving on, here are Three Core Skills that are required in order to be successful in any field of the music industry. Without mastery of these three things, your journey will be more difficult than it needs to be. These skills are as follows:

- Technical proficiency.

- A great ear.

- The ability to communicate with others.

Technical Proficiency

Having technical proficiency essentially means that you are physically capable of doing what's required of you in a given situation. Meaning if your goal is to tour with an artist as a side-person, you are capable of playing your instrument to a level that fits the situation. Or you understand how to correctly mic an acoustic guitar for a singer-songwriter you're producing.

Whatever the end goal is for your career, take stock in what you need to be able to do on a technical level to succeed at it and start working on those things now. You don't have to be a master at your craft in order to start working, but you will need enough basic technique to get whatever the job done correctly.

A Great Ear

A great ear is crucial for moving your career forward. Whether you're on stage or in the studio, being able to hear what's going on and adapting on the fly is necessary. I've been in situations where a bandleader decides to call a tune that I didn't know. Rather than just stand there on stage looking lost, I had to figure out the song in the moment, or else I wouldn't be asked to come back. The same goes for being in the studio; rarely am I given a chart for a session. As a session guitarist, it is expected of me to listen to the song once and figure out a part for it. Or, again, I wouldn't be asked to come back.

Your ears are the most precious and important piece of equipment you will ever own as a musician. It is essential that you train them to understand what it is that they are hearing. The good news is, there are many eartraining apps available for any situation.

Work on your ability to hear the difference between chord types, melodies, rhythms, and frequencies. The better your ear is, the quicker you'll pick up on what's happening in any given situation, and you'll be able to adapt to what is needed from you.

Communication

Unless your plan is to spend your career in your basement as a musical hermit, at some point you're going to have to talk with other people to further your career. Your ability to talk with, and more importantly *listen to*, your clients is essential.

Your success as a musician is going to be based on your ability to communicate with your clients about money, expectations, problems you may encounter, logistics, their feelings, and so on.

If this gives some of you anxiety—thinking about having to talk with other people about these things—you're not alone. This was the hardest thing for me to wrap my head around, and I still struggle a bit today with it. However, clear communication is key to finding work and delivering it to the best of your abilities.

One thing that helped me overcome my fear of communication with others was reading Dale Carnegie's *How to Win Friends and Influence People*. Reading this book really took my ability to communicate effectively with others to a whole new level. In turn, I was paid more for the work I was doing and respected more among my peers. It's definitely worth a look.

Music as a Service

One more thing before speaking about going out and finding work, and that is the idea of music as a service.

Unless you are a solo artist or in a band writing your own original music, most of the work you will do as a musician will be for others. Meaning, you will most likely be hired because you possess the ability to help someone else bring their musical vision to life. This is the job of a working musician. While you may be hired to bring your unique perspective or your expertise to a situation, in due course, your job is in service of someone else's ideas.

This carries over into situations where you may be writing the music yourself. For example, if you get hired to score a film, while you are the creator of the music, the music you create is in service to the film and ultimately the director's vision. If the director wants a polka band for the majority of their score, and you don't feel it's the right direction, you can voice your opinion and explain why you feel it's not correct. However, at the end of the day, if the director wants polka, you deliver the best polka you can.

It's imperative that you understand this concept, otherwise egos can be bruised and communication can break down between you and your client. This can lead to a reputation of you being difficult to work with, which is not something you want to carry around with you. Remember, as a working musician, you are being paid to help bring someone else's ideas to life because they can't do it themselves.

Finding Your Target Audience

We've discussed the core skills you need, assessed your current skill set, and discussed what it means to work as a musician. The next thing you need to do is determine who your target audience is. What group of potential clients needs the services you can provide?

To figure this out, let's break it down into three things:

- What?
- Who?
- Where?

What?

The first thing to think about is the *What*. What is it you want to be doing, and what are you capable of doing with your current skillset?

If you're still not completely sure what it is that you want to be doing, recheck that list of your current capabilities and see if anything jumps out at you.

Who?

Next, ask yourself *Who*? "Who could benefit from the skills I currently possess?" If you're a guitarist, who could use one? Singers? Producers? Cover bands?

Try to think of as many scenarios in which someone with your skill set could be useful.

Where?

Probably the most difficult of the three is figuring out where these potential clients are: Is there someplace where these people get together? Is there a Facebook/Meta group? An upcoming live event or show you know some of these people may be attending?

This can be more difficult depending on the area in which you live, but there should be at least a local music scene that you may not be aware of in your area. You just need to go digging for it.

Putting These Ideas to Work

Here's an example of putting these ideas to work: You're an engineer/ producer who is looking to find some potential clients.

What: You're a producer capable of recording, editing, and mixing, and your goal is to find some potential new clients.

Who: Who needs a producer that can record, edit, and mix? Singers, songwriters, hip-hop artists with no access to their own equipment.

Where: Where could you find some singers and songwriters? How about live shows? Open mic nights? Songwriting competitions? Song-writer organizations?

This is a good way to get a plan of attack together for your network-ing. You know what you want, for whom you're looking, and have an idea of where to run into some of these people.

The next step is getting out there and putting in the work.

Networking for the Anti-Social

The biggest obstacle a musician faces at the start of their career is the fact that no one knows who you are, and, more importantly, what you're capable of.

If you want to work, these things need to change. That means you're going to have to leave the safety of your music cave and venture out into the real world and show people that you exist.

This was probably the thing that terrified me the most when I was starting my career. I've always been a shy person, never liked parties or social gatherings. It was only my desire to work as a musician that allowed me to overcome the social anxieties that I had.

You're going to need to get active in your local music scene in order to get people to notice you. That means going to shows, sitting-in with different bands, or hanging out with groups of artists in their natural habitats.

Walking up to a complete stranger and engaging them in a conversation can be a nerve-wracking experience for the uninitiated. But have no fear. Whenever I'm out networking with strangers, I've developed a strategy that seems to work well and can ease some of the potential awkwardness that may ensue. Here it goes:

1. The first thing to remember is that you are probably not going to walk away from this conversation with a gig. That is not the purpose of engaging with a potential client. The purpose of these initial conversations is to plant a seed, nothing more. What you are trying to do is to get your name and what you do in front of as many people as possible. The idea behind this is that the more people that are aware of you and your abilities, the chances are higher that the next time they need someone like you, they'll remember. It's a game of patience. It's like fishing—you're casting as many lines as possible out there and just waiting for a bite. The more lines in the water, the higher your chances of success.

2. Next, you need to open the conversation. Make sure to keep things light while ensuring that you drop all the necessary information. Start by asking your potential client a question about themselves, keeping the attention and focus on them:

"What is it you do?"
"Did you write that song you were singing?"
"Are you performing anywhere else soon?"

One thing to remember about people, and musicians especially, is that they love to talk about themselves. So, your job is to keep the focus of the conversation on them.

If possible, start your conversation with a genuine compliment; if you just watched them perform, tell them what you liked about it. Be sincere, though; most people can see through bullshit fairly quickly.

A well-placed compliment can quickly disarm any awkwardness and keep the focus on them.

3. Once you've engaged with your potential client and kept the focus on them, an opportunity should present itself for you to drop your information. When the moment is right, you could say something like:

"My name is [blank] and I'm a [blank]."

What you're doing is giving your potential client some basic info about who you are and what it is that you do.

4. Immediately after dropping your information, turn the conversation back around to them, ask them something like:

"What are you working on?"

The idea of keeping the conversation focused completely on them is not unlike going on a first date. You don't want to be the one talking about yourself throughout the entire conversation; you want to listen to what they say and react accordingly. Keeping the focus on them as opposed to you will keep them at ease, and hopefully get them to open up a bit.

5. Once you feel that the conversation is starting to wind down, refrain from saying things like "I can help you out with that," or "We should get together and work on something." Once again, like dating, you don't want to come off too aggressive or too desperate for work. Be cool. End the conversation by handing them a business card or exchanging contact info and leave the conversation with this: "It was great meeting you, here's my card, keep me posted on what you're working on, I'd love to check it out." Then walk away.

Remember, you aren't trying to land a gig with this conversation. You are just dropping the information that you exist and you are capable of doing these things. Just putting another line in the water. Now, go and repeat this process a couple hundred times.

The more you put yourself out there, the more likely someone will remember you and thus contact you. It may take a solid month or more of networking until you start seeing results. Your success with this strategy is solely reliant on how much you hustle. Keep in mind that no one is going to call you if they don't know you exist.

When the Phone Starts Ringing or the Texts Are Flying

Fast-forward a month or so down the line, and you start to receive your first couple of calls or texts. How you move forward here is just as important as the initial networking.

For instance, someone calls/texts and wants to get together and work this coming Friday. Sounds good, right? This is what you wanted. Not so fast, though.

The situation here is that, by now, hopefully, you've been networking your butt off and met so many potential clients that they're all starting to blur together. So when you start seeing the results from your efforts, that's great, but chances are you won't remember every single person with whom you've spoken. Meaning you don't know anything about this person other than you had a conversation a month or so ago for five minutes. And now, they want to come to your workspace.

Imagine if you met some random person on the street and then just invited them into your house for the next eight to twelve hours. Doesn't sound too appealing, does it? Same with potential clients. Yes, it's great that they called, but there are some things you need to do before you commit to doing any work.

My suggestion is this: Instead of just jumping into the studio with some random person, set up a meeting somewhere outside of the workplace. Go for a coffee or drinks, sometimes even lunch. Take your potential client on a "date"; the idea behind this is that you can get a feel for what it's going to be like working for this person.

Having an initial meeting does a few things—all good. The first is that you can get a feel for how your personalities mesh. As humans, we have a pretty good built-in mechanism for identifying whether we'll get along with someone or not, and that's our gut. If you sit down with someone, normally within five minutes you can tell if this is someone you're going to get along with. Second, you can get on the same page with the client as far as what's expected on both ends. This is super important because sometimes a client has higher expectations than you can meet feasibly. And it's better to figure this out in the coffee shop rather than sitting in front of a microphone.

Don't ever agree to do a job for someone for which you know you can't deliver. Not only will you look inept, but it will ding your reputation. And your reputation is just like your credit score—it takes a lot for it to go up, but one bad mark and it takes a nosedive. So "know thyself." Have a good understanding of what you can and can't do. This will help you decide if it's the right fit for you or not.

If you know that you are incapable of delivering on the client's expectations, turning a gig down is a better solution than accepting it and failing miserably. The client will appreciate your honesty for not taking their money and failing. Even better, if you know you can't do the gig, recommend someone you know who can. This is a "boss" move. Recommending someone for a gig you've been offered that you can't do is a way to quickly build your reputation in your music scene. It shows that (a) you're an honest person who cares about getting the client what they really want, even if it means you don't do the gig personally and (b) the person to whom you recommend the gig will be grateful and most likely return the favor in the future.

However, if everything looks good—you can do the job, you get along with them, you're on the same page—great! But there is an elephant in the room that you haven't even discussed with them yet—*compensation*.

Compensation

Bringing up money is uncomfortable at first, especially if you're new to this. You may not feel that you're worthy of asking for it just yet. If that's how you feel, then ask yourself, *"When will I feel comfortable?"* Chances are it will always be a bit awkward. So rip the Band-Aid off and just dive in. The more you do this, the more you'll get used to it.

Bringing up the subject of money without sounding like an ass is even harder, but you could say something like this: *"Yeah, I'd love to help you out with this, what's your budget?"*

What's your budget? A really easy and nonchalant way of dropping that you expect to be compensated for your services. This lets the client know right away that you are assigning value to the things you bring to the table—drawing a line in the sand as it were. How they react will dictate how you are to proceed.

If they say they don't have a budget or weren't expecting to have to pay you for your time, you've just quashed that notion. And now it's up to you if you decide to proceed or not—always maintaining leverage in the negotiation.

From here, it's your decision as to if you want to continue with this client. Even though they don't have the financial compensation for you, you *do* have options. Here are three:

1. *Say no.*
   Nothing wrong with turning work down. In fact, get into the habit of saying no. It's one of the most powerful words in your vocabulary.

2. *Say yes.*
   Remember the rule "Never do anything for free, unless you want to"? This is an "unless you want to" situation. You may really like the artist and want to develop a working relationship. Perhaps it will open a door for you through one of their connections. Whatever the reason may be, the point is that *you* get to decide whether you spend your time on the project or not.

3. *Barter or trade.*
   Perhaps they don't have money but could help you out with something you need. For example, it's a female singer, and you just happen to have a track that needs a female singer. There you have it. Easy. I love the barter system and still use it to this day. You can acquire gear, favors, all sorts of things that can help you out just as much as the money would have. However, the best part about using the barter system is that you are getting used to the idea of getting something for your time, and you are teaching your clients that you need them to come to the table with something if they want you to provide your services.

So now you see that even with no budget, you still have options—all viable, all useful.

Compensation Part II (How Much?)

Now, time to talk about money.

This is always a tricky situation. How much is too much? What is this service worth? Trying to figure out your rates is always complicated at first. Here are some thoughts:

For instance, the client has $1,000 dollars to pay you for your services. They need some recording, editing, and a light mixing on one track. Sounds good, right? This is what is known as working for a "flat rate." While there is nothing wrong with flat rates in most situations, you run into an issue when you are talking about music-related services. Meaning, most artists are never satisfied with their work. It's normal. So if you take $1,000 to finish someone's track, when that track is finished is now at the behest of the artist. That means it could take six months for the artist to be "satisfied" with the work. And now you've "outrun the money." That $1,000 isn't worth so much now.

It's not advisable to do flat rates unless certain parameters are met. The main one being the project has a *hard deadline*—it has a firm end date. For instance, you get hired to score a TV commercial. In all probability, that commercial needs to be finished and on air by a certain date. Meaning that once it's released, you're done. This works the same with a live gig. You get paid a flat amount of money to perform. The night's over, you get paid. Boom. Done. So unless there is a defined end point to the project, it's unadvisable to take a flat rate.

A better use of your time is to get in the habit of charging by the hour. This way, no matter how indecisive the client is or how long they take to be "happy," you get compensated for your time. If the artist wants to talk about their hi-hats for three hours, cool; you still get compensated for that time.

Finding Your Rate

How you figure out what to charge is always tricky. Do you charge based on your skill level? Your experience? The going rate in your area?

Here's a little formula that can help you get an idea of where to start, and it goes like this:

The first thing you need to figure out is what your monthly "survival" budget is. How much money do you require every month to get by? Rent is paid, car is paid, all your bills are taken care of, but you don't have much wiggle room. Say that number is $1,500 per month.

Now, what you're going to do is double that:

$$\$1{,}500 \times 2 = \$3{,}000$$

Remember, you're not trying to just "survive"; you're trying to "thrive." So doubling what you need is a good place to start.

Next, you're going to figure how many working days in a month—Monday through Friday. Five days a week, four weeks in a month = 20 days:

$$\$3{,}000 / 20 \text{ days} = \$150/\text{day}$$

Now, divide $150 per day by a standard workday of eight hours.

$$\$150 / 8 \text{ hours} = \$18.75/\text{hour}$$

Okay, you've come up with $18.75 per hour. Now, here's the thing: This is not what you charge clients. What this is, is your *minimum* wage. This is your bottom line. Meaning you cannot work for less than $18.75 per hour; this is your super bro/sis rate.

The idea behind this is just like a car dealership. The dealership knows what the car costs, but they mark up the sticker price. So the customer comes in and tries to negotiate that sticker price down, while never knowing what the actual bottom line is.

What you do is when someone asks you how much you charge, you remember your bottom line and mark up your sticker price. I like to say that you should double it, so maybe start your negotiation at $40/hour. Your client may respond by saying that that's too expensive. You now have the ability to say something like *"You know, I like the project, I like you. Tell you what. How about $30 dollars an hour?"* Just like the car dealer, you make the client feel like they're getting a special deal. All the while, you are making a living wage for yourself but never going below your bottom line. Everyone's bottom line will be different, and your bottom line will shift with changes in your expenses. Use it as a reference for the lowest price for which you can comfortably work.

HOURLY RATE CALCULATOR

Monthly "Survival" Budget _____ × 2 = _____ (thrive budget)

Thrive Budget _____ ÷ 20 (days) = _____ (daily rate)

Daily Rate _____ ÷ 8 (hours) = _____ (baseline hourly rate)

Baseline Hourly Rate _____ × 2 = _____ (negotiable starting rate)

Negotiable Starting Hourly Rate
$ _____

Figure 3.1. Hourly Rate Calculator
Author

Getting Paid

Now, actually getting the money you are owed can be an issue with some clients. Some you'll never have a problem with. And those are the ones you want to keep around. But those that hassle you about pay can be a problem. Here are some thoughts about different methods of getting your money.

I always like to give new clients the benefit of the doubt once. And only once. If they don't pay me what was agreed, or at all, I never deal with them again.

Getting Paid Up Front

This one is tricky, especially if you're charging hourly, as you don't know how long you'll be working on the project. However, for live gigs or session work, this could be an option.

Getting a Deposit

Same problem as getting paid up front if you're working hourly. With some live gigs you can do this, especially weddings and the like.

Contracts

While I am an advocate of having a contract with all of my clients, it is in no way a guarantee that you will be able to collect your money, especially if you're dealing with anything under $10,000. For instance, in California, if you have a contract with a client and they fail to pay you and the money owed is less than $7,500 (check the laws in your state), you'll end up in what is known as "small claims court." If you don't know what an immense hassle may be, you're lucky.

Put it this way: You may end up spending more time and money than what is owed to you chasing it down through small claims court.

So what's the best solution?

How I Get Paid Every Time

I have discovered a foolproof way of getting paid for my work in the studio every single time. And it's a very simple solution: First of all, I expect to be paid at the end of each day. That way, the bill doesn't get so large as to scare the client from paying in large chunks at a time. However, what do I do to ensure payment? I give the client nothing until I'm paid. Not a bounce nor a rough mix, a file, an MP3—nothing.

Once you give a client the work that you've done, you've lost all leverage in the situation. And now you're chasing them to pay you. That's a position in which you never want to be. Hold on to all the work and tell the client that you'll be happy to give them everything you've done; they just need to pony up what they owe. Always works.

You can add some stipulations into your contracts with these clients that will further ensure payment. These things are discussed in a later chapter.

CHAPTER FOUR
INDEPENDENT CONTRACTOR

CONTRACT

Jane_Kelly/Getty Images

Once your networking starts to bear fruit and you start to take on your first clients, the way you will conduct your business should be very different than any other job you may have had in the past. You may have heard the terms work for hire, freelance, and sole proprietor; they all mean the same thing—*independent contractor.*

For most of the work you take on as a professional musician, you will be considered an independent contractor. What does that mean? Basically, it means you work for yourself.

However, as with anything, there are good things and bad things involved with this type of work. First, here are the good things:

- You're your own boss.

- You set your own schedule.

- You dictate how much you charge.

- You can choose your clients.

All good things. But there is a flip side. Now, the not so good things:

- Inconsistent work

- Inconsistent money

- No benefits. Health and retirement benefits are up to you.

- Harder to get financing (loans, mortgages, car loans, etc.)

- Taxes

Pros

Taking the reins and going into business for yourself can be very liberating.

- You don't have someone looking over your shoulder, telling you what to do and when to do it.

- You're the master of your own destiny. If you feel like taking a week off and doing absolutely nothing, there is no one to stop you.

- The money you make is yours and yours alone.

- You set the terms and conditions of payment.

- You have the choice to work with certain clients and turn down others.

Cons

The hardest thing about going into business for yourself is typically going to be the *start-up*.

- If you are used to getting a steady paycheck to rely on every week, giving that up can be a bit disconcerting at first.

- Networking takes time to yield results, and it can be downright scary to jump into the unknown and give up a sure thing. This is the point that many will give up and return to a "safe" job.

- If you're coming from a job that offers benefits like health and dental insurance, losing that can be a real punch in the gut too. Same goes for things like retirement benefits.

- Trying to get credit or a home loan becomes almost nightmarish when you work for yourself.

I remember one time trying to buy a car. I told the dealer with great pride that I was a professional music producer. He then said to me that he will need to see the previous five years of my financial records, tax returns, and bank statements. The funny thing was that I had enough cash in my accounts to buy the car outright, three times over. But nope, he needed to see that I was making enough money working on my own before they gave me a loan. Here's the best part. When they pulled my credit, it showed that I taught at a college. Even though it was only two days a week and a mere pittance of the money that I make on my own, the dealer says, "Oh, you teach at a college?"

"Yeah," I said.

"Never mind about the financial records, we're good."

And I got the financing, just like that.

As I've mentioned before, people not in our business tend to have a low view of "music people." Remember Beyoncé or broke?

Last, but certainly not least, are taxes. If you've enjoyed getting a W-2 at the end of the year and filing your taxes with a DIY software, then waiting patiently for your tax return to show up, say goodbye to all of that. As an independent contractor, you'll be lucky if you can get by with owing as little as possible. However, there are certain things you can do with taxes to ease a bit of the burden.

Taxes

As an independent contractor, you become responsible for keeping track of your income and spending. When you have a regular job, that's taken care of for you with your W-2 form. One of the things you are able to do is take advantage of something known as a "deduction," or "write-off." What is a write-off?

"A write-off is a deduction in the value of earnings by the amount of an expense or loss. When businesses file their income tax return, they are able to write off expenses incurred to run the business and subtract them from their revenue to determine their taxable income."

To clarify, this is a fancy way of saying that if you spend money on anything related to your business, you can offset your taxable income or revenue (money you make). For example:

- You make $10,000 running your business this year. Your current tax rate would be about 12%. You would owe around $1,200 in taxes with no write-offs.

- However, if you bought a new computer this year as an upgrade for your business and spent $2,000 on it, you could deduct the $2,000 for the computer from the $10,000 you earned.

- So $10,000 (revenue) minus $2,000 (business expense) = $8,000 (deducted revenue)

What you've done is knocked your taxable income (revenue) down from $10,000 to $8,000 (deducted revenue). Now you will pay taxes on only $8,000 instead of $10,000.

You can use write-offs to great effect to help keep the money you owe in check.

If you've never done this before, it's a good idea to speak to a tax professional to get an idea of what you can and can't do.

So what counts as a write-off, or business expense? Anything you spend money on that relates to your business. For example, start with music gear:

- Computers
- Software (Pro Tools, plug-ins, updates, samplers, soft synths)
- Instruments
- Accessories for instruments (strings, picks, tuners, pedals)
- Speakers

- Cables

- Computer desk and chair

- Microphones

- Outboard equipment

- And on and on and on

Use your imagination. If it cost you money and you use it to generate more money, it counts.

Some other things you can use as write-offs:

- *Business lunches/dinners.* Remember your "client date"? You can write off up to 50% of those; however, deductions are subject to the whims of the government.

- *Gas or miles on your car.* If you use your car to drive to gigs or to sessions, you can choose one or the other, but not both—just pick the one that will save you the most money. Again, subject to the whims of the government.

- *Depreciation.* Once again, if you use your car for your "business," you can write off the amount of value your car loses every year. You can find the past and current value of your car on Kelly Blue Book—www.kbb.com.

- *Rent.* If you work from home and have a dedicated space, you can take what is known as the "Home Office Deduction." This allows you to write off a portion of your rent and utilities based on the square footage your home office occupies, up to 50%. For instance, if your home office occupies 20% of your entire home's square footage, you can write off 20% of your rent and utilities. Homeowners can also write off mortgage insurance and utilities.

When filing your taxes, you will most likely add up all of your expenses and submit them as an "itemized" deduction. Once again, you are urged to consider hiring a professional tax preparer if you've never done this. They are experts in their field and know what you can and can't do.

Plus, the money you spend on an accountant can be written off the following year as a business expense.

Another important thing to do is to save your receipts, *all* of your receipts. You will need to save up to five years of your expenses, just in case you get an audit. The IRS will want to see all of your expenses, and any receipts you can't provide may incur a penalty.

Keeping track of hundreds of tiny pieces of paper can seem a bit overwhelming. Fortunately, there are many ways we can keep track of them with relative ease. There are apps for your mobile phones, pocket scanners, or other devices. Here is a $3 solution to keep track of everything. All you need to do is take a trip to a dollar store and buy three things:

- One pack of manila folders

- One box of letter-sizes envelopes

- One Sharpie

On the manila folder, write the year, for instance "2022." Then on each of the twelve smaller letter-sized envelopes write the twelve months of the year. "Jan 2022," "Feb 2022," "Mar 2022," and so on, until you have an individual envelope for every month of the year.

Keep one of these small envelopes in your car every month. That way, whenever you get gas, buy lunch, or pay for parking, just put the receipt directly into the envelope. At the end of the month, remove that month's envelope and place it in the larger manila envelope. Then place the next month's envelope in the car and repeat the cycle. By keeping your receipts in individual monthly envelopes, you're able to keep track of your monthly expenses with relative ease. So at the end of the year, you have twelve individual envelopes with all your monthly expenses right in front of you. It's a simple solution, but it absolutely works.

1099

It was mentioned earlier that when you work for yourself, you will no longer have the luxury of receiving a W-2 at the end of the year. You may, however, be introduced to a new piece of paper called a *1099*.

Depending on how tax savvy your clients are, they may make you fill out a form called an I-9. On this form, you will put all of your personal information, such as your name, address, and social security number. (*I personally don't like giving my social security number [SS#] to anyone, because I don't trust that they will be as careful with it as I am. There is something else you can put on this form in lieu of your* social security, *but I'll explain that later.*)

What a 1099 amounts to is that it offers your clients a way to deduct "you" as a business expense. You typically won't receive one from them if you make under $600. But if you do, it shows the IRS that you were paid a specific amount as an independent contractor, and you are responsible for paying the income tax for it. Very cut and dry, so don't freak out if a client wants to give you one. It's all part of working for yourself.

Attention:

Copy A of this form is provided for informational purposes only. Copy A appears in red, similar to the official IRS form. The official printed version of Copy A of this IRS form is scannable, but the online version of it, printed from this website, is not. Do **not** print and file copy A downloaded from this website; a penalty may be imposed for filing with the IRS information return forms that can't be scanned. See part O in the current General Instructions for Certain Information Returns, available at www.irs.gov/form1099, for more information about penalties.

Please note that Copy B and other copies of this form, which appear in black, may be downloaded and printed and used to satisfy the requirement to provide the information to the recipient.

To order official IRS information returns, which include a scannable Copy A for filing with the IRS and all other applicable copies of the form, visit www.IRS.gov/orderforms. Click on Employer and Information Returns, and we'll mail you the forms you request and their instructions, as well as any publications you may order.

Information returns may also be filed electronically using the IRS Filing Information Returns Electronically (FIRE) system (visit www.IRS.gov/FIRE) or the IRS Affordable Care Act Information Returns (AIR) program (visit www.IRS.gov/AIR).

See IRS Publications 1141, 1167, and 1179 for more information about printing these tax forms.

9595   ☐ VOID   ☐ CORRECTED

PAYER'S name, street address, city or town, state or province, country, ZIP or foreign postal code, and telephone no.		1 Rents $	OMB No. 1545-0115	Miscellaneous Information
		2 Royalties $	2021 Form **1099-MISC**	
		3 Other income $	4 Federal income tax withheld $	**Copy A** For **Internal Revenue Service Center**
PAYER'S TIN	RECIPIENT'S TIN	5 Fishing boat proceeds $	6 Medical and health care payments $	File with Form 1096.
RECIPIENT'S name		7 Payer made direct sales totaling $5,000 or more of consumer products to a recipient for resale ☐	8 Substitute payments in lieu of dividends or interest $	For Privacy Act and Paperwork Reduction Act Notice, see the **2021 General Instructions for Certain Information Returns.**
Street address (including apt. no.)		9 Crop insurance proceeds $	10 Gross proceeds paid to an attorney $	
City or town, state or province, country, and ZIP or foreign postal code		11 Fish purchased for resale $	12 Section 409A deferrals $	
Account number (see instructions)	FATCA filing requirement ☐ 2nd TIN not. ☐	13 Excess golden parachute payments $	14 Nonqualified deferred compensation $	
		15 State tax withheld $ $	16 State/Payer's state no.	17 State income $ $

Form **1099-MISC**   Cat. No. 14425J   www.irs.gov/Form1099MISC   Department of the Treasury - Internal Revenue Service

Do Not Cut or Separate Forms on This Page — Do Not Cut or Separate Forms on This Page

Figure 4.1. Form 1099-MISC. To download this form, go to https://www.irs.gov/pub/irs-pdf/f1099msc.pdf.

U.S. Government

PAYER'S name, street address, city or town, state or province, country, ZIP or foreign postal code, and telephone no.		**1** Rents $	OMB No. 1545-0115	
		2 Royalties $	20**21** Form **1099-MISC**	**Miscellaneous Information**
		3 Other income $	**4** Federal income tax withheld $	**Copy 1**
PAYER'S TIN	RECIPIENT'S TIN	**5** Fishing boat proceeds $	**6** Medical and health care payments $	**For State Tax Department**
RECIPIENT'S name		**7** Payer made direct sales totaling $5,000 or more of consumer products to recipient for resale ☐	**8** Substitute payments in lieu of dividends or interest $	
Street address (including apt. no.)		**9** Crop insurance proceeds $	**10** Gross proceeds paid to an attorney $	
City or town, state or province, country, and ZIP or foreign postal code		**11** Fish purchased for resale $	**12** Section 409A deferrals $	
Account number (see instructions)	FATCA filing requirement ☐	**13** Excess golden parachute payments $	**14** Nonqualified deferred compensation $	
		15 State tax withheld $ $	**16** State/Payer's state no.	**17** State income $ $

Form **1099-MISC**   www.irs.gov/Form1099MISC   Department of the Treasury - Internal Revenue Service

---

PAYER'S name, street address, city or town, state or province, country, ZIP or foreign postal code, and telephone no.		**1** Rents $	OMB No. 1545-0115	
		2 Royalties $	20**21** Form **1099-MISC**	**Miscellaneous Information**
		3 Other income $	**4** Federal income tax withheld $	**Copy B**
PAYER'S TIN	RECIPIENT'S TIN	**5** Fishing boat proceeds $	**6** Medical and health care payments $	**For Recipient**
RECIPIENT'S name		**7** Payer made direct sales totaling $5,000 or more of consumer products to recipient for resale ☐	**8** Substitute payments in lieu of dividends or interest $	This is important tax information and is being furnished to the IRS. If you are required to file a return, a negligence penalty or other sanction may be imposed on you if this income is taxable and the IRS determines that it has not been reported.
Street address (including apt. no.)		**9** Crop insurance proceeds $	**10** Gross proceeds paid to an attorney $	
City or town, state or province, country, and ZIP or foreign postal code		**11** Fish purchased for resale $	**12** Section 409A deferrals $	
Account number (see instructions)	FATCA filing requirement ☐	**13** Excess golden parachute payments $	**14** Nonqualified deferred compensation $	
		15 State tax withheld $ $	**16** State/Payer's state no.	**17** State income $ $

Form **1099-MISC**   (keep for your records)   www.irs.gov/Form1099MISC   Department of the Treasury - Internal Revenue Service

Instructions for Recipient

Recipient's taxpayer identification number (TIN). For your protection, this form may show only the last four digits of your social security number (SSN), individual taxpayer identification number (ITIN), adoption taxpayer identification number (ATIN), or employer identification number (EIN). However, the payer has reported your complete TIN to the IRS.

Account number. May show an account or other unique number the payer assigned to distinguish your account.

FATCA filing requirement. If the FATCA filing requirement box is checked, the payer is reporting on this Form 1099 to satisfy its account reporting requirement under chapter 4 of the Internal Revenue Code. You may also have a filing requirement. See the Instructions for Form 8938.

Amounts shown may be subject to self-employment (SE) tax. Individuals should see the Instructions for Schedule SE (Form 1040). Corporations, fiduciaries, or partnerships must report the amounts on the appropriate line of their tax returns.

Form 1099-MISC incorrect? If this form is incorrect or has been issued in error, contact the payer. If you cannot get this form corrected, attach an explanation to your tax return and report your information correctly.

Box 1. Report rents from real estate on Schedule E (Form 1040). However, report rents on Schedule C (Form 1040) if you provided significant services to the tenant, sold real estate as a business, or rented personal property as a business. See Pub. 527.

Box 2. Report royalties from oil, gas, or mineral properties; copyrights; and patents on Schedule E (Form 1040). However, report payments for a working interest as explained in the Schedule E (Form 1040) instructions. For royalties on timber, coal, and iron ore, see Pub. 544.

Box 3. Generally, report this amount on the "Other income" line of Schedule 1 (Form 1040) and identify the payment. The amount shown may be payments received as the beneficiary of a deceased employee, prizes, awards, taxable damages, Indian gaming profits, or other taxable income. See Pub. 525. If it is trade or business income, report this amount on Schedule C or F (Form 1040).

Box 4. Shows backup withholding or withholding on Indian gaming profits. Generally, a payer must backup withhold if you did not furnish your TIN. See Form W-9 and Pub. 505 for more information. Report this amount on your income tax return as tax withheld.

Box 5. Shows the amount paid to a fishing boat crew member who is considered by the operator to be self-employed. Self-employed individuals must report this amount on Schedule C (Form 1040). See Pub. 334.

Box 6. For individuals, report on Schedule C (Form 1040).

Box 7. If checked, consumer products totaling $5,000 or more were sold to you for resale, on a buy-sell, a deposit-commission, or other basis. Generally, report any income from your sale of these products on Schedule C (Form 1040).

Box 8. Shows substitute payments in lieu of dividends or tax-exempt interest received by your broker on your behalf as a result of a loan of your securities. Report on the "Other income" line of Schedule 1 (Form 1040).

Box 9. Report this amount on Schedule F (Form 1040).

Box 10. Shows gross proceeds paid to an attorney in connection with legal services. Report only the taxable part as income on your return.

Box 11. Shows the amount paid for the purchase of fish from any person engaged in the trade or business of catching fish. See the instructions for your tax return for reporting this income.

Box 12. May show current year deferrals as a nonemployee under a nonqualified deferred compensation (NQDC) plan that is subject to the requirements of section 409A plus any earnings on current and prior year deferrals.

Box 13. Shows your total compensation of excess golden parachute payments subject to a 20% excise tax. See your tax return instructions for where to report.

Box 14. Shows income as a nonemployee under an NQDC plan that does not meet the requirements of section 409A. Any amount included in box 12 that is currently taxable is also included in this box. Report this amount as income on your tax return. This income is also subject to a substantial additional tax to be reported on Form 1040, 1040-SR, or 1040-NR. See the instructions for your tax return.

Boxes 15–17. Show state or local income tax withheld from the payments.

Future developments. For the latest information about developments related to Form 1099-MISC and its instructions, such as legislation enacted after they were published, go to *www.irs.gov/Form1099MISC*.

Free File. Go to *www.irs.gov/FreeFile* to see if you qualify for no-cost online federal tax preparation, e-filing, and direct deposit or payment options.

☐ CORRECTED (if checked)

PAYER'S name, street address, city or town, state or province, country, ZIP or foreign postal code, and telephone no.		1 Rents $	OMB No. 1545-0115	Miscellaneous Information
		2 Royalties $	2021 Form **1099-MISC**	
		3 Other income $	4 Federal income tax withheld $	**Copy 2**
PAYER'S TIN	RECIPIENT'S TIN	5 Fishing boat proceeds $	6 Medical and health care payments $	**To be filed with recipient's state income tax return, when required.**
RECIPIENT'S name		7 Payer made direct sales totaling $5,000 or more of consumer products to recipient for resale ☐	8 Substitute payments in lieu of dividends or interest $	
Street address (including apt. no.)		9 Crop insurance proceeds $	10 Gross proceeds paid to an attorney $	
City or town, state or province, country, and ZIP or foreign postal code		11 Fish purchased for resale $	12 Section 409A deferrals $	
Account number (see instructions)	FATCA filing requirement ☐	13 Excess golden parachute payments $	14 Nonqualified deferred compensation $	
		15 State tax withheld $ $	16 State/Payer's state no.	17 State income $ $

Form **1099-MISC**   www.irs.gov/Form1099MISC   Department of the Treasury - Internal Revenue Service

Figure 4.1. *Continued*

☐ VOID	☐ CORRECTED			

PAYER'S name, street address, city or town, state or province, country, ZIP or foreign postal code, and telephone no.	**1 Rents** $	OMB No. 1545-0115	**Miscellaneous Information**
	2 Royalties $	20**21** Form **1099-MISC**	
	3 Other income $	**4 Federal income tax withheld** $	**Copy C** **For Payer**
PAYER'S TIN	RECIPIENT'S TIN	**5 Fishing boat proceeds** $	**6 Medical and health care payments** $	
RECIPIENT'S name		**7 Payer made direct sales totaling $5,000 or more of consumer products to recipient for resale ☐**	**8 Substitute payments in lieu of dividends or interest** $	For Privacy Act and Paperwork Reduction Act Notice, see the **2021 General Instructions for Certain Information Returns.**
Street address (including apt. no.)		**9 Crop insurance proceeds** $	**10 Gross proceeds paid to an attorney** $	
City or town, state or province, country, and ZIP or foreign postal code		**11 Fish purchased for resale** $	**12 Section 409A deferrals** $	
Account number (see instructions)	FATCA filing requirement ☐	2nd TIN not. ☐	**13 Excess golden parachute payments** $	**14 Nonqualified deferred compensation** $	
			15 State tax withheld $ $	**16 State/Payer's state no.**	**17 State income** $ $

Form **1099-MISC**   www.irs.gov/Form1099MISC   Department of the Treasury - Internal Revenue Service

Instructions for Payer

To complete Form 1099-MISC, use:

• The 2021 General Instructions for Certain Information Returns, and

• The 2021 Instructions for Forms 1099-MISC and 1099-NEC.

To complete corrected Forms 1099-MISC, see the 2021 General Instructions for Certain Information Returns.

To order these instructions and additional forms, go to *www.irs.gov/Form1099MISC*.

Caution: Because paper forms are scanned during processing, you cannot file Forms 1096, 1097, 1098, 1099, 3921, or 5498 that you print from the IRS website.

Due dates. Furnish Copy B of this form to the recipient by January 31, 2022. The due date is extended to February 15, 2022, if you are reporting payments in box 8 or 10.

File Copy A of this form with the IRS by February 28, 2022, if you file on paper, or by March 31, 2022, if you file electronically.

To file electronically, you must have software that generates a file according to the specifications in Pub. 1220. The IRS does not provide a fill-in form option for Copy A.

Need help? If you have questions about reporting on Form 1099-MISC, call the information reporting customer service site toll free at 866-455-7438 or 304-263-8700 (not toll free). Persons with a hearing or speech disability with access to TTY/TDD equipment can call 304-579-4827 (not toll free).

Employment Eligibility Verification
Department of Homeland Security
U.S. Citizenship and Immigration Services

USCIS
Form I-9
OMB No. 1615-0047
Expires 10/31/2022

▶ START HERE: Read instructions carefully before completing this form. The instructions must be available, either in paper or electronically, during completion of this form. Employers are liable for errors in the completion of this form.

ANTI-DISCRIMINATION NOTICE: It is illegal to discriminate against work-authorized individuals. Employers **CANNOT** specify which document(s) an employee may present to establish employment authorization and identity. The refusal to hire or continue to employ an individual because the documentation presented has a future expiration date may also constitute illegal discrimination.

Section 1. Employee Information and Attestation *(Employees must complete and sign Section 1 of Form I-9 no later than the **first day of employment**, but not before accepting a job offer.)*

Last Name *(Family Name)*	First Name *(Given Name)*	Middle Initial	Other Last Names Used *(if any)*

Address *(Street Number and Name)*	Apt. Number	City or Town	State	ZIP Code

Date of Birth *(mm/dd/yyyy)*	U.S. Social Security Number	Employee's E-mail Address	Employee's Telephone Number
	☐☐☐ - ☐☐ - ☐☐☐☐		

I am aware that federal law provides for imprisonment and/or fines for false statements or use of false documents in connection with the completion of this form.

I attest, under penalty of perjury, that I am (check one of the following boxes):

☐ 1. A citizen of the United States

☐ 2. A noncitizen national of the United States *(See instructions)*

☐ 3. A lawful permanent resident   (Alien Registration Number/USCIS Number): _____

☐ 4. An alien authorized to work   until (expiration date, if applicable, mm/dd/yyyy): _____
Some aliens may write "N/A" in the expiration date field. *(See instructions)*

Aliens authorized to work must provide only one of the following document numbers to complete Form I-9:
An Alien Registration Number/USCIS Number OR Form I-94 Admission Number OR Foreign Passport Number.

QR Code - Section 1
Do Not Write In This Space

1. Alien Registration Number/USCIS Number: _____
   OR
2. Form I-94 Admission Number: _____
   OR
3. Foreign Passport Number: _____
   Country of Issuance: _____

Signature of Employee	Today's Date *(mm/dd/yyyy)*

Preparer and/or Translator Certification (check one):
☐ I did not use a preparer or translator.   ☐ A preparer(s) and/or translator(s) assisted the employee in completing Section 1.
(Fields below must be completed and signed when preparers and/or translators assist an employee in completing Section 1.)

I attest, under penalty of perjury, that I have assisted in the completion of Section 1 of this form and that to the best of my knowledge the information is true and correct.

Signature of Preparer or Translator	Today's Date *(mm/dd/yyyy)*

Last Name *(Family Name)*	First Name *(Given Name)*

Address *(Street Number and Name)*	City or Town	State	ZIP Code

🛑 *Employer Completes Next Page* 🛑

Figure 4.2.   Form I-9 Employment Eligibility Verification. Department of Homeland Security. U.S. Citizenship and Immigration Services. To download this form, go to https://www.uscis.gov/sites/default/files/document/forms/i-9-paper-version.pdf.
U.S. Government

Employment Eligibility Verification
Department of Homeland Security
U.S. Citizenship and Immigration Services

USCIS
Form I-9
OMB No. 1615-0047
Expires 10/31/2022

Section 2. Employer or Authorized Representative Review and Verification

(Employers or their authorized representative must complete and sign Section 2 within 3 business days of the employee's first day of employment. You must physically examine one document from List A OR a combination of one document from List B and one document from List C as listed on the "Lists of Acceptable Documents.")

Employee Info from Section 1	Last Name *(Family Name)*	First Name *(Given Name)*	M.I.	Citizenship/Immigration Status

List A	OR	List B	AND	List C
Identity and Employment Authorization		Identity		Employment Authorization

List A	List B	List C
Document Title	Document Title	Document Title
Issuing Authority	Issuing Authority	Issuing Authority
Document Number	Document Number	Document Number
Expiration Date *(if any) (mm/dd/yyyy)*	Expiration Date *(if any) (mm/dd/yyyy)*	Expiration Date *(if any) (mm/dd/yyyy)*

Document Title		
Issuing Authority	Additional Information	QR Code - Sections 2 & 3 Do Not Write In This Space
Document Number		
Expiration Date *(if any) (mm/dd/yyyy)*		
Document Title		
Issuing Authority		
Document Number		
Expiration Date *(if any) (mm/dd/yyyy)*		

Certification: I attest, under penalty of perjury, that (1) I have examined the document(s) presented by the above-named employee, (2) the above-listed document(s) appear to be genuine and to relate to the employee named, and (3) to the best of my knowledge the employee is authorized to work in the United States.

The employee's first day of employment *(mm/dd/yyyy):* _____ *(See instructions for exemptions)*

Signature of Employer or Authorized Representative	Today's Date *(mm/dd/yyyy)*	Title of Employer or Authorized Representative
Last Name of Employer or Authorized Representative	First Name of Employer or Authorized Representative	Employer's Business or Organization Name

Employer's Business or Organization Address *(Street Number and Name)*	City or Town	State	ZIP Code

Section 3. Reverification and Rehires *(To be completed and signed by employer or authorized representative.)*

A. New Name *(if applicable)*			B. Date of Rehire *(if applicable)*
Last Name *(Family Name)*	First Name *(Given Name)*	Middle Initial	Date *(mm/dd/yyyy)*

C. If the employee's previous grant of employment authorization has expired, provide the information for the document or receipt that establishes continuing employment authorization in the space provided below.

Document Title	Document Number	Expiration Date *(if any) (mm/dd/yyyy)*

I attest, under penalty of perjury, that to the best of my knowledge, this employee is authorized to work in the United States, and if the employee presented document(s), the document(s) I have examined appear to be genuine and to relate to the individual.

Signature of Employer or Authorized Representative	Today's Date *(mm/dd/yyyy)*	Name of Employer or Authorized Representative

LISTS OF ACCEPTABLE DOCUMENTS
All documents must be UNEXPIRED

Employees may present one selection from List A
or a combination of one selection from List B and one selection from List C.

LIST A		LIST B		LIST C
Documents that Establish Both Identity and Employment Authorization	**OR**	**Documents that Establish Identity**	**AND**	**Documents that Establish Employment Authorization**
1. U.S. Passport or U.S. Passport Card		1. Driver's license or ID card issued by a State or outlying possession of the United States provided it contains a photograph or information such as name, date of birth, gender, height, eye color, and address		1. A Social Security Account Number card, unless the card includes one of the following restrictions:
2. Permanent Resident Card or Alien Registration Receipt Card (Form I-551)				(1) NOT VALID FOR EMPLOYMENT
				(2) VALID FOR WORK ONLY WITH INS AUTHORIZATION
3. Foreign passport that contains a temporary I-551 stamp or temporary I-551 printed notation on a machine-readable immigrant visa		2. ID card issued by federal, state or local government agencies or entities, provided it contains a photograph or information such as name, date of birth, gender, height, eye color, and address		(3) VALID FOR WORK ONLY WITH DHS AUTHORIZATION
4. Employment Authorization Document that contains a photograph (Form I-766)		3. School ID card with a photograph		2. Certification of report of birth issued by the Department of State (Forms DS-1350, FS-545, FS-240)
5. For a nonimmigrant alien authorized to work for a specific employer because of his or her status:		4. Voter's registration card		3. Original or certified copy of birth certificate issued by a State, county, municipal authority, or territory of the United States bearing an official seal
a. Foreign passport; and		5. U.S. Military card or draft record		
		6. Military dependent's ID card		
b. Form I-94 or Form I-94A that has the following:		7. U.S. Coast Guard Merchant Mariner Card		4. Native American tribal document
(1) The same name as the passport; and		8. Native American tribal document		5. U.S. Citizen ID Card (Form I-197)
(2) An endorsement of the alien's nonimmigrant status as long as that period of endorsement has not yet expired and the proposed employment is not in conflict with any restrictions or limitations identified on the form.		9. Driver's license issued by a Canadian government authority		6. Identification Card for Use of Resident Citizen in the United States (Form I-179)
		For persons under age 18 who are unable to present a document listed above:		7. Employment authorization document issued by the Department of Homeland Security
6. Passport from the Federated States of Micronesia (FSM) or the Republic of the Marshall Islands (RMI) with Form I-94 or Form I-94A indicating nonimmigrant admission under the Compact of Free Association Between the United States and the FSM or RMI		10. School record or report card		
		11. Clinic, doctor, or hospital record		
		12. Day-care or nursery school record		

Examples of many of these documents appear in the Handbook for Employers (M-274).

Refer to the instructions for more information about acceptable receipts.

Figure 4.2. *Continued*

Best Buy or Craigslist

Here's a question: You're in the market for a new laptop. You have two options for purchasing it—one is from Best Buy (or a similar big retailer), the other is from some guy on Craigslist. Pretend that there is nothing wrong with either one of them. They cost exactly the same. Which one would you go for?

It's assumed that you would buy from Best Buy. Why? Probably because you associate Best Buy with a reputation. You recognize the brand, and that brand comes with a certain amount of credibility and protection that a Craigslist person just doesn't.

So why bring this up?

Because when you strike out on your own as an independent contractor, your brand, your reputation, is your name. This is not to sound offensive whatsoever, but when you start out, no one knows your name or of what you're capable.

You're just some random person. And when you have clients deciding with whom they are going to work, this can become a factor.

So what you want to do is transform yourself from being thought of as some random person on Craigslist, to being seen as a little more like Best Buy. The saying "fake it 'til you make it" applies here. The perception a potential client has of you is everything when they're deciding on whether or not to hire you. If they think that you're just some person in their bedroom offering your services, chances are they may be a little turned off to hiring you. What you're going to do is alter that perception by making yourself seem a little more like a legitimate business, even though you may still be working out of your bedroom.

What's in a Name?

First things first. You need to rebrand yourself as a business as opposed to an individual, and that requires creating a brand that people will associate with your work.

If you think of all the huge corporations that you know and see every day, they all started somewhere. For instance, take a company like McDonald's: When you're driving down the road and you see a giant golden "M," you immediately know what that is. Even if you rarely eat there, you could probably recite half the menu from memory because of their ads. That is what is called "brand recognition."

When the first McDonald's opened in 1953, no one knew what it was. The original name of McDonald's was "McDonald's Hamburgers." No one at the time would know what McDonald's did if they hadn't put it right there on the sign—they sell hamburgers. As their reputation grew over the years, they were able to drop the modifiers that described what they did, until they ended up with the giant "M." Their reputation began to precede them.

So just like McDonald's, you need to come up with a name that describes what it is you can do for your clients. One example in choosing a name is to use something personal and add a modifier to it that explains what you do. For instance:

- Your name is Jane Smith

- You are a mixing engineer

You could call your business "JS Mixing," or "Smith Post Group," "Jane's World Studios," or the like.

The point is that you choose a name that is simple and descriptive. When you're out networking and you meet a potential client, saying you run the "Smith Post Group" sounds much cooler than just giving someone your name. The perception you create is that you have your shit together and are operating as a true professional.

One thing my grandfather taught me when I was young, was that when you're dealing with people you want to KISS them—keep it simple, stupid.

If you allow people to come up with their own ideas about who you are and what you do, chances are they may come up with the wrong impression. So with the name you choose, you don't allow for any interpretation other than the one you give. This keeps the perception a potential client has of you exactly where you want it to be.

Once you've decided on a name, the next thing you have to do is set yourself up to accept payment under said name. It's not as simple as just going to the bank and opening a business account. You actually have to take some steps to set yourself up as a legit business. There is nothing more embarrassing than getting a client to hire you as "Smith Post

Group," but when it comes time to write the check, or make the electronic payment, or swipe the card, and you charge them as "Jane Smith," the illusion is shattered. It's like going to the checkout at a store and the cashier says to pay her instead of the company. Not a good move.

Here are a few things you can do to remedy this.

Getting the Business Up and Running

Once you've settled on a name, the first thing you need to do, and I can't stress this enough—you need to get the actual domain name for a website. So you want to use "Smith Post Group" as your business name? Make sure that www.smithpostgroup.com is available. Not smithpostgroup. net, smithpostgroup.org, or smith-post-group.com. Remember, keep it simple, stupid. If you have to explain to a potential client how they can find you on the internet, you've already lost.

Once you come up with a name, go immediately to a website design format like www.godaddy.com or www.squarespace.com and search to see if it's available. If it's not, keep adjusting your name until you find one that works.

Most search engines default to searching for the .com websites. So by choosing anything else, you run the risk of being on page three of Google, which everyone knows is the wasteland of Google.

Make it easy to remember and easy to spell. There was a study done by NPR a few years ago about how long most people will spend searching for something new on Google. They found most people will spend only about three seconds before they give up. Therefore, three seconds is your window. Make sure they can find you. If your website is too clever or convoluted, you're done before you start.

Once you get the domain straightened out, the next thing is to create a website. This is your portal to the world. This is where people can seek you out for your services. It is your online business card and résumé all rolled into one. You may also want to grab all the social media handles for your business name too. Have them all linked to your one central hub website.

The good news these days is that it is extremely easy to set up a professional-looking website. There are numerous websites that offer professional-looking templates for creating a website using drag and drop mechanics, so you no longer need to hire a professional programmer. Get this done first.

Setting Up a DBA

The next thing you need to do is set yourself up as a business, so you can accept payment. The easiest and cheapest solution is to set up what is called a DBA, or "doing business as." What a DBA does is it allows you to work as an independent contractor while using a made-up name. So the only difference between working as "Jane Smith," the independent contractor, and "Smith Post Group" is that the DBA is the name. Everything else stays the same.

Setting up a DBA is relatively easy but requires a few trips to city hall and normally around $200–$250 (business expense). Although it varies from state to state, what you need to do and how much it costs are usually similar.

First thing you do is what is called a "fictitious name" search, where the name you want to use as a business will be searched to see if anyone else is using it. If it comes back clean, you're good to go. If someone else is using the name, you will have to adjust the name you want to use until it comes back that no one is using it.

Once you get approval on the name, the next thing you will do is register it as a business operating within your city. Once again, the price for doing this varies, depending on where you are located. You will probably have to get some forms notarized by a notary public. They can be found typically at banks or city hall for these purposes; if not, many pack-and-ship stores like a UPS store tend to have a notary or two working there.

At some point, you will be given the option to acquire what is known as an "EIN number." An EIN, or Employment Identification Number, is a unique nine-digit number assigned by the IRS to businesses. You will definitely want to get one; here's why: Remember the 1099 form discussed earlier? When you fill out your I-9 form, instead of submitting your personal social security number, you can use your EIN and it serves the same purpose. However, your EIN cannot be used to steal your identity or commit fraud. It is associated with you as a business, not personally. So it's basically an extra layer of personal protection when doing business.

The last step, once again depending on where you are, is running a print ad for four weeks stating your intention to do business in your city. This ad doesn't have to be anything fancy. You can run it in something like a community periodical for around $5.

It's a bit of an old school way of doing things, but it's what's required.

Once all of these things are done, you'll be able to go to your local bank and set up a business account under your new business name. This means that you will be able to accept payment as a business and also pay for expenses as a business. You can now get a credit card swiper for your mobile devices, checks with your business name on them, and a company debit card. All in all, you will look super legit, even if you're still working out of your bedroom.

Turning Your DBA into an LLC

At some point, you may want to expand your business turning it into an LLC. What's the difference between a DBA and an LLC? Remember, working as a DBA, you are still considered an independent contractor—you are your business. That means that you and your business's fates are intertwined. If you have a client that decides to sue your business, they are in effect, suing you.

LLC stands for limited liability company. The major difference is with an LLC, you and your business become separate. That means that if your business is sued, only your business is at risk. You are not personally liable for your business. LLCs offer an added layer of protection, but it comes at a price. They are generally much more expensive to operate, constituting annual fees that can cost as much as $1,500 a year or more.

Setting one up is very similar to setting up a DBA but much more expensive. It's not recommended to start one up until you have established enough work to warrant the expense.

Online Legal Services

Doing all this paperwork and driving around just to get your business up and running can be exhausting. Thanks to the modern joys of technology, there are many online services available that can take the headache out of setting up your business. There are sites that provide all online legal services all from the comfort of your home. Spend some time researching some of these services and see if one is the right fit for what you're looking to do. They may be more expensive than doing it yourself, but that's the price you pay for convenience and deeper knowledge.

Accepting Payment

Once you have your website and business account set up, you're good to go for accepting payments from your clients. There are many different ways to get paid for your services, here are a few of them.

Invoices

First things first. You need to get accustomed to writing and sending invoices. An invoice is essentially an itemized bill and receipt that you provide to your clients to show a breakdown of the services you have provided and how much each one cost. There are many templates on the web that you can take and customize to your liking, as well as many apps and programs that can generate them automatically for you. The layout can be whatever you choose, but there is certain information that needs to be in any invoice to keep things on the up-and-up.

- Your business information, such as your address, phone number, and email
- Your client's business information for billing purposes
- An itemized breakdown of what services were performed and how much each cost
- Invoice date
- Date you expect payment
- Invoice number for your records
- A subtotal for all services
- Any additional taxes or fees (such as the 2.9% PayPal fee)
- Final total
- Additional notes

Company Name
(Or your business name)

INVOICE

Street Address
City, ST ZIP Code
Phone: Phone Fax: Fax

INVOICE # 100
DATE: DATE

TO:
Recipient Name
Company Name
Street Address
City, ST ZIP Code
Phone: Phone

COMMENTS OR SPECIAL INSTRUCTIONS:
(Add any special requests from your client, make sure to spell out and be specific as to what the job entails)

Terms: (This is where you state when you should receive payment, it's best to put "Due Upon Receipt")

QUANTITY	DESCRIPTION	UNIT PRICE	TOTAL
(# of hours)	(Here you will go into detail about the services you provide)	(Your hourly rate)	(# of hours **X** hourly rate)

	SUBTOTAL	
	SALES TAX/EXTRA FEES	(This is where you can add any extra fees)
	TOTAL DUE	(Final Total)

Make all checks payable to Company Name
If you have any questions concerning this invoice, contact: Name, Phone, Email

THANK YOU FOR YOUR BUSINESS!

Figure 4.3. Sample Invoice
Author

Cash

Cash is king! If a client pays you in cash, you're all good. Make sure you still provide an invoice that states that they have paid you for your services, for their records, as well as yours.

It may be tempting to keep the cash "under the table" and not claim it on your income taxes. Don't make this a habit.

Credit Cards

Accepting payment with a credit card is almost as good as cash, mainly because it will either clear right away or not. You can use services like PayPal, Square, or Venmo to accept credit card payments. However, PayPal charges a fee for all business transactions. If someone requests to pay me via PayPal, I tend to tack on the fee on top of what they owe me, so I still get paid my full amount. Same thing goes if you get a card reader for your phone; there is typically a fee associated with using it. You can add this fee to your invoice so your client understands that they are being charged for the convenience of using their credit card.

Checks

Yes, they still exist. *(I still have many clients that like to pay via checks.)* The only danger with getting paid with a check is if it doesn't clear. Best advice would be to withhold any files or work that you have done until the check clears. *(Most of the time I give first-time clients the benefit of the doubt when it comes to checks. If they write me a bad check, I will never accept another one from them. Cash or card from that day forward.)* The reason is because if you deposit a bad check, not only do you not get the money for the work you did, but your bank will probably charge you a bounced check fee—that could be upward of $50. So tread carefully when it comes to checks.

A Final Thought on Getting Paid

At some point in your career, you will encounter a client who is "unhappy" with the work you provide. This is normal, and it will happen. Remember that music is subjective. *(One thing I've learned from all the artists that I've dealt with over the years is this: They are never totally "happy" with their work.)* Some will try to use their "unhappiness" as an excuse not to pay you. If you did the job to the best of your ability and fulfilled every expectation that you had discussed with your client prior to working together, then your client's "happiness" should not be a factor in your getting paid. The saying "Great art is never finished, it's just abandoned" fits here.

A big misconception that most clients have is that they are paying for a *product*, when in actuality, they are paying for a *service*. This is also why we get paid by the hour instead of a flat rate. Clients tend to have a difficult time making up their minds about this or that; they will never be satisfied fully with the work that they do. (It's normal for any artist to want to keep pushing for perfection, but not at the expense of reason.)

It has zero to do with your talent. It's just human nature. With this in mind, when a client states their "unhappiness," try your best to show them that what you have worked on together is good. See if you can talk them down from that cliff. You'd be surprised how effective it is to just hear them out and logically discuss the situation. However, there are still the ones who can't be moved, and nothing you say will deter them.

Now the flip side: If you messed up and you know it, then they have every right to withhold payment from you. Own up to it and do everything in your power to fix "your" mistake. Be accountable; do what you say. If you can't abide by that, then you won't last very long in this industry.

Remember, you're dealing with artists. They can be finnicky. Just always carry yourself with integrity and accountability; talk through any problems you may have with a client. The solution is normally something simple where both parties walk away happy.

A big misconception that most clients have is that they are paying for a product, when in actuality, they are paying for a service.

CHAPTER FIVE
PROTECTING YOUR WORK

ileezhun/Getty Images

I f I were to look back at my career and all the mistakes that I've made over the years, none would stick out more than the lesson I learned working for a major producer on hit records. When I got to Los Angeles, I didn't know a soul. I was starting from scratch; I had to build my networks of gigs and players from the ground up.

As luck would have it, I ended up in the right place at the right time and landed a gig with a very prominent producer who was working with some of the biggest artists of the day. I remember meeting him and the sheer joy I felt when he asked me to come to his studio and play on some tracks. I felt that after being in LA for only six months, I had achieved the thing I set out to do. I was a professional session musician.

Everything started out great. I was making somewhere around $1,000 per day, playing on big records, meeting everybody under the sun. Life was good for about a month. After that first month, the producer approached me and asked me to join his team full-time and become a writer. "That's where the real money is!" he said to me. I looked at his fancy cars and the million-dollar studio we were working out of day after day and thought "I should listen to him; he obviously knows what's up."

After agreeing to join up full-time as a writer/session musician, I figured he would eventually explain to me how everything worked. But that day never came. All the while, he didn't have to pay me for my session work anymore because I was a writer and being a writer was better than just being a session guy.

Over the next four years, that was my job. I spent nearly every day in that studio, sometimes working sixteen- to twenty-hour days. I had no social life, no friends outside of my work environment, and no other work opportunities because I was at the studio all day, every day.

I remember two distinct instances that shook me out of this routine. The first was coming home from an all-day session working with one of the most popular artists of the day and seeing a three day or quit notice on the door to my apartment. I hadn't been able to get my rent together for the month yet. It hit me that something was wrong with this scenario. I was just hanging out and helping people who drive Bentleys and Ferraris make more money for their music empires, yet here I was looking at a possible eviction from my little Hollywood apartment. Something wasn't adding up.

The next thing I started noticing was when I would be driving somewhere or at the store and hear the music coming over the radio. I would hear these songs playing and think to myself, "Where have I heard this before?" until I realized, I knew exactly where—I had helped write it. I recognized my guitar playing instantly. And because I had, at that point, worked on hundreds of tracks, it was easy to lose track (no pun intended) of what I had created.

Eventually, I confronted the producer about this, to which he replied, "Did you write on those?" Taken aback, I said, "Well, I'm the only guy that's here seven days a week that sits next to you every day and can actually play an instrument. So, yeah. I think I may have had something to do with the writing of these songs."

"Don't worry, I'll take care of it," he said.

I'm not sure whether or not I was being naïve or the fact that I didn't want to push too hard on the subject. But I let it go, thinking that he would do right by me and take care of everything. Man, was I wrong—it kept happening. Eventually, I contacted a lawyer I had met through working with him and asked what my options were.

When I told her my story about what was going on, she said to me, "It's a common occurrence in the industry to take advantage of the ignorance of relatively talented newcomers." I asked her what my options were at this point, to which she replied, "There are two options, and you won't like either one of them."

"Option one, you can sue him."

"Great! Let's do that!" I replied.

She then proceeded to tell me how things would play out if I went down that road: "First, you'll need a lawyer. And judging by the fact that you can barely pay your rent, I doubt you can afford one. He has a high-powered multi-million-dollar music attorney. They will bury you in legal fees before anyone can hear your case."

My heart sank.

She continued, "Let's say you do successfully take him to court, and you even win. You better be happy with the money you get because that's it. No one in this town will work with you again because you're the guy that sues. You'll be a pariah. People won't want you around because they're afraid that if you sued one producer, you may sue another."

Okay, that option sucks. "What's my other option?"

"Take it as a really expensive lesson," she said.

After four years of my life spent helping a millionaire stay a million-aire while getting nothing in return, I was justifiably disheartened with the music industry. All the royalties and credits that should have been mine were gone and out of reach. I started packing my things for my inevitable return home, defeated.

But I'm also pretty stubborn. I don't like being taken advantage of and felt like the best revenge would be to overcome this obstacle and become successful, regardless.

I took it as a lesson. I made a point to learn where I went wrong so no one could ever pull a fast one on me again. Here's what I learned.

Copyright

First of all, what is copyright, and what does it mean?

Copyright grants the legal right for the creator of an original work to use and distribute it as they see fit. Basically, it means, *you make it—you own it.*

Copyright can cover a wide-ranging array of things other than music, such as books, films, and video games, and any intellectual property (IP) that you create and is original is considered protected by copyright.

If someone uses your work without your permission, you could sue them for what is known as copyright infringement.

Copyright can be a little confusing because of the way the law is written. I've seen my fair share of artists get screwed over because they weren't clear on what it was and when it goes into effect.

When Is Something Considered under the Protection of Copyright?

Copyright takes effect the moment a work is considered tangible. What does "tangible" mean? It means "perceptible by touch." Essentially, the minute it goes from being an idea in your head to existing in the physical world, written on paper or recorded onto your computer or your phone, it is protected in that moment.

Normally, this wouldn't pose much of an issue, but here's a worst-case scenario example of where this may become an issue.

When you talk about a hit song, a lot of times most people don't realize how much money one can make while their song is sitting at Number One on the charts. Put it this way, it's somewhat like winning the lottery. You've probably heard stories of lotto winners saying how all of a sudden, they had a lot more relatives than they did before they won. People tend to crawl out of the woodwork when you're dealing with large sums of money. Because a hit song can generate so much money, you may deal with the same problems.

This is based on a true story. The names have been altered, but you'll get the gist:

A very popular artist was writing and recording a song one night in a North Hollywood recording studio. At some point during the evening, she ran out of her, we'll say, "inspiration."

Wanting the session to continue, she had a friend of a friend call up an individual who could provide some more inspiration. Once he arrived at the studio and everyone was feeling inspired, the artist thought he was a pretty cool dude and asked if he wanted to continue hanging out. The inspiration dealer obliged. As they all hung out through the night, the artist finished writing what would end up being one of her biggest hit songs to date—a lot of money would be made.

Once the song was released and climbing the charts, her management got a letter from a law firm representing the inspiration dealer. He was claiming that he helped contribute to the creation of the song and was entitled to a percentage of the ownership and profits.

Sounds crazy right? Did he have a claim?

Believe it or not, a judge ruled that he did. The only question asked of the artist and her writers was, "Was he there?" In order not to perjure themselves, they agreed that he was there as they were writing the song. And because of the way the law is written, he was there when it became a tangible thing. Plus, the artist couldn't prove that if he weren't there, she would have written the same song. So guess what? They had to give him a piece of the song. It may have been only 5%, but still, that's fairly good for just hanging out in the room.

Now you may be asking yourself, "Why didn't the engineer or the other staff members at the studio pull the same stunt?" That's because the engineer was either an independent contractor or was on the payroll of the studio. Being an independent contractor, you typically waive any rights to anything on which you're working in lieu of payment. The same for the employees at the studio. They relinquish any rights to anything that goes on in the studio by accepting a paycheck or signing a contract with the studio. "Inspiration" guy was neither.

Most professional writing sessions should be run like a tight ship. Only the people who are writers and the independent contractors are typically allowed in as to avoid these types of situations.

This is something of which you should be mindful and never forget. Because you never know if that song you're working on is going to turn into something.

When I ran my studio in Venice, California, I had a really simple and effective way of dealing with this. I worked with a lot of hip-hop artists, and hip-hop artists tend to roll pretty deep with their entourages. So I had a sign-in sheet that everyone except the artist with whom I was working had to fill out. It was really simple: print name, sign name, date. However, there was a paragraph at the top of the page that read something like this:

"By signing and dating this form, I the undersigned, waive all rights and claims of ownership to any music created at this location (*location*), on this date (*date*), and at this time (*time*)."

Really simple, but highly effective. Basically, if you didn't sign, you weren't allowed in. I did this primarily as a precaution because my studio was doing a lot of commercial and advertising work. And if someone tried to pull the same "I was there" BS, it could not only ruin my reputation but also that of the advertising firm I was working with as well as the company we were working for. All around, a bad situation.

So out of an abundance of caution, those were the rules.

How Long Does Copyright Last?

For works published after 1977, copyright lasts for the life of the author plus seventy years in the United States. If you write a song with a friend, the copyright will last for the life of the last living author plus seventy years. So if you write a song with a friend and get hit by a bus tomorrow, your copyright will be protected until your friend gets hit by a bus plus seventy years in the United States. After an author's death, the rights will go to whomever the author has chosen to control their estate. If no one is named, it will typically go to one's next of kin.

What Constitutes a Music Copyright?

A music copyright is considered by an identifiable melody or lyric or both. A chord progression or a beat cannot be copyrighted. Sorry for that news.

However, things have been getting dicey over the last decade with lawsuits like the Robin Thicke vs. Marvin Gaye estate. There were claims that the song "Blurred Lines" sounded very similar to Marvin Gaye's "Got to Give It Up." Even though there was no blatant melody or lyric infringement, a jury saw fit to award the Gaye estate with over $7 million.

This has opened up numerous lawsuits, many of them considered frivolous. Anything that even slightly resembles something else that's out there is considered fair game now.

Registering a Copyright

Although copyright protection is instant, you still should formalize it by registering your work with the U.S. Office of Copyright. You can do this at www.copyright.gov. You can upload directly either the sheet music or an MP3 of your work. Currently, to copyright a song formally is going to cost you around $35 per track. Things can get expensive quickly. Once it's uploaded, you're good to go. Even while your copyright application is still processing, it is legitimately protected by the government.

Form PA
For a Work of Performing Arts
UNITED STATES COPYRIGHT OFFICE

REGISTRATION NUMBER

PA   PAU

EFFECTIVE DATE OF REGISTRATION

Month   Day   Year

DO NOT WRITE ABOVE THIS LINE. IF YOU NEED MORE SPACE, USE A SEPARATE CONTINUATION SHEET.

1

TITLE OF THIS WORK ▼

PREVIOUS OR ALTERNATIVE TITLES ▼

NATURE OF THIS WORK ▼ See instructions

2

a

NAME OF AUTHOR ▼

DATES OF BIRTH AND DEATH
Year Born ▼   Year Died ▼

Was this contribution to the work a "work made for hire"?
☐ Yes
☐ No

AUTHOR'S NATIONALITY OR DOMICILE
Name of Country
OR { Citizen of _____
Domiciled in _____

WAS THIS AUTHOR'S CONTRIBUTION TO THE WORK
Anonymous? ☐ Yes ☐ No
Pseudonymous? ☐ Yes ☐ No
If the answer to either of these questions is "Yes," see detailed instructions.

NATURE OF AUTHORSHIP Briefly describe nature of material created by this author in which copyright is claimed. ▼

NOTE
Under the law, the "author" of a "work made for hire" is generally the employer, not the employee (see instructions). For any part of this work that was "made for hire" check "Yes" in the space provided, give the employer (or other person for whom the work was prepared) as "Author" of that part, and leave the space for dates of birth and death blank.

b

NAME OF AUTHOR ▼

DATES OF BIRTH AND DEATH
Year Born ▼   Year Died ▼

Was this contribution to the work a "work made for hire"?
☐ Yes
☐ No

AUTHOR'S NATIONALITY OR DOMICILE
Name of Country
OR { Citizen of _____
Domiciled in _____

WAS THIS AUTHOR'S CONTRIBUTION TO THE WORK
Anonymous? ☐ Yes ☐ No
Pseudonymous? ☐ Yes ☐ No
If the answer to either of these questions is "Yes," see detailed instructions.

NATURE OF AUTHORSHIP Briefly describe nature of material created by this author in which copyright is claimed. ▼

c

NAME OF AUTHOR ▼

DATES OF BIRTH AND DEATH
Year Born ▼   Year Died ▼

Was this contribution to the work a "work made for hire"?
☐ Yes
☐ No

AUTHOR'S NATIONALITY OR DOMICILE
Name of Country
OR { Citizen of _____
Domiciled in _____

WAS THIS AUTHOR'S CONTRIBUTION TO THE WORK
Anonymous? ☐ Yes ☐ No
Pseudonymous? ☐ Yes ☐ No
If the answer to either of these questions is "Yes," see detailed instructions.

NATURE OF AUTHORSHIP Briefly describe nature of material created by this author in which copyright is claimed. ▼

3

a

YEAR IN WHICH CREATION OF THIS WORK WAS COMPLETED This information must be given in all cases.
_____ Year

b

DATE AND NATION OF FIRST PUBLICATION OF THIS PARTICULAR WORK
Complete this information ONLY if this work has been published.
Month _____ Day _____ Year _____ Nation

4

See instructions before completing this space.

COPYRIGHT CLAIMANT(S) Name and address must be given even if the claimant is the same as the author given in space 2. ▼

TRANSFER If the claimant(s) named here in space 4 is (are) different from the author(s) named in space 2, give a brief statement of how the claimant(s) obtained ownership of the copyright. ▼

DO NOT WRITE HERE OFFICE USE ONLY

APPLICATION RECEIVED

ONE DEPOSIT RECEIVED

TWO DEPOSITS RECEIVED

FUNDS RECEIVED

MORE ON BACK ▶ · Complete all applicable spaces (numbers 5-9) on the reverse side of this page.
· See detailed instructions.   · Sign the form at line 8.

DO NOT WRITE HERE
Page 1 of _____ pages

Figure 5.1a. Sample U.S. Copyright Form PA page 1. To download this form, go to https://www.copyright.gov/forms/formpa.pdf.

U.S. Government

DO NOT WRITE ABOVE THIS LINE. IF YOU NEED MORE SPACE, USE A SEPARATE CONTINUATION SHEET.

PREVIOUS REGISTRATION Has registration for this work, or for an earlier version of this work, already been made in the Copyright Office?

☐ Yes ☐ No If your answer is "Yes," why is another registration being sought? (Check appropriate box.) ▼ If your answer is No, do **not** check box A, B, or C.

a. ☐ This is the first published edition of a work previously registered in unpublished form.

b. ☐ This is the first application submitted by this author as copyright claimant.

c. ☐ This is a changed version of the work, as shown by space 6 on this application.

If your answer is "Yes," give **Previous Registration Number** ▼   **Year of Registration** ▼

5

DERIVATIVE WORK OR COMPILATION Complete both space 6a and 6b for a derivative work; complete only 6b for a compilation.

Preexisting Material Identify any preexisting work or works that this work is based on or incorporates. ▼

Material Added to This Work Give a brief, general statement of the material that has been added to this work and in which copyright is claimed. ▼

a 6 b

See instructions before completing this space.

DEPOSIT ACCOUNT If the registration fee is to be charged to a Deposit Account established in the Copyright Office, give name and number of Account.

Name ▼   **Account Number** ▼

CORRESPONDENCE Give name and address to which correspondence about this application should be sent. Name/Address/Apt/City/State/Zip ▼

Area code and daytime telephone number   (   )   Fax number   (   )

Email

a 7 b

CERTIFICATION* I, the undersigned, hereby certify that I am the

Check only one ▶
{
☐ author
☐ other copyright claimant
☐ owner of exclusive right(s)
☐ authorized agent of _____
}

Name of author or other copyright claimant, or owner of exclusive right(s) ▲

of the work identified in this application and that the statements made by me in this application are correct to the best of my knowledge.

Typed or printed name and date ▼ If this application gives a date of publication in space 3, do not sign and submit it before that date.

_____ Date _____

Signature (X) ▼

☞ x _____

8

Certificate will be mailed in window envelope to this address:	Name ▼
	Number/Street/Apt ▼
	City/State/Zip ▼

YOU MUST:
· Complete all necessary spaces
· Sign your application in space 8

SEND ALL 3 ELEMENTS IN THE SAME PACKAGE:
1. Application form
2. Nonrefundable filing fee in check or money order payable to *U.S. Copyright Office*
3. Deposit material

MAIL TO:
Library of Congress
Copyright Office-PA
101 Independence Avenue SE
Washington, DC 20559-6000

9

*17 U.S.C. §506(e): Any person who knowingly makes a false representation of a material fact in the application for copyright registration provided for by section 409, or in any written statement filed in connection with the application, shall be fined not more than $2,500.

Form PA–Full   Printed: 05/2019   Printed on recycled paper

Figure 5.1b. Sample U.S. Copyright Form PA page 2. To download this form, go to https://www.copyright.gov/forms/formpa.pdf.

U.S. Government

If you do have a large catalog of music, one option available to you is to register your songs as a "volume" or "compilation." If they're all your compositions, no problem. If you make an album where you write fifteen of sixteen songs, but you wrote the sixteenth song with a friend, you will have to pay a separate fee for that sixteenth song, but you could register the other fifteen together.

Once It's Done, It's Done

Understanding how copyright law works is very important when it comes to collaborating with others. A lot of my students are making beats and "renting" (licensing) them out to artists. It is advised to be aware that even though they may be making a little money doing this, it's a recipe for disaster.

The reason is, because copyright is instant—when you write a song with someone, you've essentially baked a music cake. If you brought the eggs and your writing partner brought the sugar, once they're combined, it's impossible to separate them back into their individual parts. It exists as it is.

A lot of you may like to try out different writers for your music, but the first iteration of the song is essentially the last. If you have sent your tracks to several different writers and the fourth writer ends up writing a hit, everyone who came before could have a claim to the copyright. Remember that you can't quantify creativity. You could argue that your music led the writer in a certain lyrical direction that they wouldn't have normally gone if your music wasn't there in the first place. It's a sticky situation.

I once worked with an artist who was new to LA, and we ended up writing what I feel is one of the best songs I've ever written. I knew we wouldn't have a problem placing it and making some money off it. I asked her repeatedly if she understood how everything worked according to ownership and rights. She said she understood. I told her it may take a minute, but this will make us both some money.

She wasn't very patient. I got a call from her two months later, saying another artist wants to use the lyrics for their song. I explained to her that she can't do that, which she took as my telling her "You can't do this . . . to me." Quite the contrary, I explained that she legally could not sell the lyrics to our song without my permission. We made a music baby. It was done. After a lot of swearing and name-calling from her, I ended up with a completely useless track. I wouldn't be able to license the song without her permission; therefore, we couldn't make any money off the song. Rather than take the risk of ruining my reputation by trying to license a song I didn't have full permission for, I killed the track. It's been sitting on my hard drive ever since.

So to be clear, it may not seem like an issue trying a bunch of different writers on your tracks; chances are (no offense) nothing will happen with them. But should lightning strike, you will want to make sure that you have all your legal ducks in a row so you don't run into problems.

The easiest way to avoid these problems is to just write a new song with everyone. You're creative enough. Plus, the more songs you write, the better you'll get at it.

Public Domain

After a copyright expires, the work becomes what is known as "public domain." Essentially, that means that anyone has the right to re-create said work and license or sell it at their discretion. Now, don't get all excited *thinking* that you can freely sample things that are public domain; there's a catch (see "A Note about Using Samples in Your Work" below).

Two Copyrights

When dealing with music and copyright, there are actually two separate copyrights involved: The first is the song itself referred to as the *composition*. You write the song, you own it. However, there is a second copyright that goes along with it, and that is on the recording of the song—referred to as the *master* or *master recording* (or sound recording).

What this means is that even though Beethoven's *Fifth Symphony* is considered public domain, you can't sample or use a recording of it for your own benefit because the recording most likely still falls under copyright protection. You can create your own recording and use that to your heart's desire. However, you cannot use someone else's recording (without permission).

Form SR
For a Sound Recording
UNITED STATES COPYRIGHT OFFICE

REGISTRATION NUMBER

_____

SR _____ SRU _____

EFFECTIVE DATE OF REGISTRATION

Month _____ Day _____ Year _____

DO NOT WRITE ABOVE THIS LINE. IF YOU NEED MORE SPACE, USE A SEPARATE CONTINUATION SHEET.

1

TITLE OF THIS WORK ▼

PREVIOUS, ALTERNATIVE, OR CONTENTS TITLES (CIRCLE ONE) ▼

2

a

NAME OF AUTHOR ▼

DATES OF BIRTH AND DEATH ▼
Year Born ▼   Year Died ▼

Was this contribution to the work a "work made for hire"?
☐ Yes
☐ No

AUTHOR'S NATIONALITY OR DOMICILE
Name of Country
OR { Citizen of ▶ _____
Domiciled in ▶ _____

WAS THIS AUTHOR'S CONTRIBUTION TO THE WORK
Anonymous?   ☐ Yes   ☐ No
Pseudonymous? ☐ Yes   ☐ No
If the answer to either of these questions is "Yes," see detailed instructions.

NATURE OF AUTHORSHIP   Briefly describe nature of material created by this author in which copyright is claimed. ▼

NOTE

Under the law, the "author" of a "work made for hire" is generally the employer, not the employee (see instructions). For any part of this work that was "made for hire," check "Yes" in the space provided, give the employer (or other person for whom the work was prepared) as "Author" of that part, and leave the space for dates of birth and death blank.

b

NAME OF AUTHOR ▼

DATES OF BIRTH AND DEATH ▼
Year Born ▼   Year Died ▼

Was this contribution to the work a "work made for hire"?
☐ Yes
☐ No

AUTHOR'S NATIONALITY OR DOMICILE
Name of Country
OR { Citizen of ▶ _____
Domiciled in ▶ _____

WAS THIS AUTHOR'S CONTRIBUTION TO THE WORK
Anonymous?   ☐ Yes   ☐ No
Pseudonymous? ☐ Yes   ☐ No
If the answer to either of these questions is "Yes," see detailed instructions.

NATURE OF AUTHORSHIP   Briefly describe nature of material created by this author in which copyright is claimed. ▼

c

NAME OF AUTHOR ▼

DATES OF BIRTH AND DEATH ▼
Year Born ▼   Year Died ▼

Was this contribution to the work a "work made for hire"?
☐ Yes
☐ No

AUTHOR'S NATIONALITY OR DOMICILE
Name of Country
OR { Citizen of ▶ _____
Domiciled in ▶ _____

WAS THIS AUTHOR'S CONTRIBUTION TO THE WORK
Anonymous?   ☐ Yes   ☐ No
Pseudonymous? ☐ Yes   ☐ No
If the answer to either of these questions is "Yes," see detailed instructions.

NATURE OF AUTHORSHIP   Briefly describe nature of material created by this author in which copyright is claimed. ▼

3

a YEAR IN WHICH CREATION OF THIS WORK WAS COMPLETED
This information must be given in all cases.
Year ▶

b DATE AND NATION OF FIRST PUBLICATION OF THIS PARTICULAR WORK
Complete this information ONLY if this work has been published.
Month ▶ _____ Day ▶ _____ Year ▶ _____
Nation ▶

4

a COPYRIGHT CLAIMANT(S) Name and address must be given even if the claimant is the same as the author given in space 2. ▼

See instructions before completing this space.

b TRANSFER If the claimant(s) named here in space 4 is (are) different from the author(s) named in space 2, give a brief statement of how the claimant(s) obtained ownership of the copyright. ▼

APPLICATION RECEIVED

ONE DEPOSIT RECEIVED

TWO DEPOSITS RECEIVED

FUNDS RECEIVED

DO NOT WRITE HERE
OFFICE USE ONLY

MORE ON BACK ▶ · Complete all applicable spaces (numbers 5-9) on the reverse side of this page.
· See detailed instructions.   · Sign the form at line 8.

DO NOT WRITE HERE
Page 1 of _____ pages

Figure 5.2a.   Sample U.S. Copyright Form SR page 1. To download this form, go to https://www.copyright.gov/forms/formsr.pdf.

U.S. Government

DO NOT WRITE ABOVE THIS LINE. IF YOU NEED MORE SPACE, USE A SEPARATE CONTINUATION SHEET.

PREVIOUS REGISTRATION Has registration for this work, or for an earlier version of this work, already been made in the Copyright Office?

❑ Yes ❑ No If your answer is "Yes," why is another registration being sought? (Check appropriate box) ▼

a. ❑ This work was previously registered in unpublished form and now has been published for the first time.

b. ❑ This is the first application submitted by this author as copyright claimant.

c. ❑ This is a changed version of the work, as shown by space 6 on this application.

If your answer is "Yes," give: **Previous Registration Number** ▼   **Year of Registration** ▼

5

DERIVATIVE WORK OR COMPILATION

Preexisting Material Identify any preexisting work or works that this work is based on or incorporates. ▼

a

Material Added to This Work Give a brief, general statement of the material that has been added to this work and in which copyright is claimed. ▼

b

6

See instructions before completing this space.

DEPOSIT ACCOUNT If the registration fee is to be charged to a deposit account established in the Copyright Office, give name and number of account.

   Name ▼   Account Number ▼

a

CORRESPONDENCE Give name and address to which correspondence about this application should be sent. Name/Address/Apt/City/State/Zip ▼

b

   Area code and daytime telephone number   (   )   Fax number   (   )

   Email

7

CERTIFICATION* I, the undersigned, hereby certify that I am the

Check only one ▼

❑ author   ❑ owner of exclusive right(s)

❑ other copyright claimant   ❑ authorized agent of _____

                        Name of author or other copyright claimant, or owner of exclusive right(s) ▲

of the work identified in this application and that the statements made by me in this application are correct to the best of my knowledge.

Typed or printed name and date ▼ If this application gives a date of publication in space 3, do not sign and submit it before that date.

_____ Date _____

       Signature ▼

8

9

*17 U.S.C. §506(e): Any person who knowingly makes a false representation of a material fact in the application for copyright registration provided for by section 409, or in any written statement filed in connection with the application, shall be fined not more than $2,500.

Form SR-Full Rev: 05/2019 Printed on recycled paper

Figure 5.2b. Sample U.S. Copyright Form SR page 2. To download this form, go to https://www.copyright.gov/forms/formsr.pdf.

U.S. Government

A sound recording copyright is signified by using a circle with a *P* (℗) in the middle to indicate "phonograph."

Generally, the owner of the master is the person or company that financed the recording. *If you're signed to a record label, then they own the master recording.*

Whoever owns the master can then do as they wish with that version of the song. They can license it to whomever they choose with little to no say from the writer of the song.

When a master recording is licensed for visual media, there is typically a fee associated with it called a "synchronization fee," or sync fee. A sync fee is money paid up front for the use of the recording by a third party (i.e., TV, film, or video game). The amount of a sync fee varies and generally depends on how popular the song is. The writer rarely sees any of this money unless they also own their master (most labels are keeping the entire sync fees these days; some split them, but most don't).

Don't be disheartened by this. As a writer, you are entitled to something else much better.

Final word. You're better off taking inspiration from a sample, recreating the vibe, and making your own version. You'll avoid a lot of headaches down the road.

A NOTE ABOUT USING SAMPLES IN YOUR WORK

My advice: If samples are not from a royalty-free sample library—don't use them. If you must, you have to obtain permission from the writer, the owner of the master, and the owner of the copyright of the song. If it's a popular song, it can cost you a fortune.

Don't think you can get away with changing it enough that someone won't notice it buried in your track; you'd be surprised how quickly one can recognize them.

Here's an example of when we got caught for using a track without permission. Back in the day, the left and right sides of the mixes would contain certain instruments. The left side may have just had the drums and the bass, while the right side had the guitar and the horns. The producer mentioned previously took the right side of an old Delfonics' tune.

He grabbed this really cool guitar riff from the right side of the recording, sped it up, and layered it into his beat, then finished the song and released it. Not even a month after it was released, we received a letter from the Delfonics' publisher saying we either needed to pull the track or give them $50,000 cash as well as all the publishing for the song. Moral of the story: don't think you can get away with using a sample without permission.

If you're planning on placing a track in a movie, TV show, or commercial, another thing to keep in mind—most music supervisors won't even consider using something with a sample. The reason is, if it gets used and it hasn't been fully cleared, not only are you in trouble but so is the parent company of the show that used it. So that will cost a lot of people their jobs.

Royalties

As the owner of an original work, you are entitled to license and sell it at your discretion. One of the best things about being a writer is that whenever someone decides to utilize your work, you are able to earn income from its use known as a "royalty."

There are two types of royalties of which you should be aware, and each does something a little different.

Mechanical Royalty

A *mechanical royalty* is generated whenever a song is purchased physically, downloaded, or streamed digitally via an on-demand streaming platform such as Spotify. It's normally paid to the owner of the copyright or the publisher.

The current mechanical royalty rate for physical recordings and permanent music downloads is 9.1 cents, the rate is set by the Library of Congress's Royalty Copyright Board.

Mechanical royalties are paid to the owner(s) of the composition. Most often the royalty comes from whomever controls the master and is paid to either the songwriters, the publishers, or both. The songwriter is guaranteed at least 50% of the mechanical royalty considered the *writer's share*, whereas the publisher collects the other half, or *publisher's share*. If you are a self-published writer, you can collect 100% of the mechanical.

In the United States, the Harry Fox Agency and the MLC (Mechanical Licensing Collective) are responsible for the collection and distribution of mechanical royalties.

Performance Royalty

This is the royalty you should concern yourself with most. A performance royalty is generated from the public performance of a work. Every song you hear on the radio, the TV, a commercial, electronic media, a movie, or a sporting event is generating a performance royalty. Based on how often it is played publicly, a hit song can generate hundreds of thousands of dollars a year in performance royalties.

Performing Rights Organizations (PROs)

In order to collect a performance royalty, you need to first be a member of a performing rights organization. In the United States, currently there are ASCAP, BMI, SESAC, Global Music Rights, and Sound Exchange (and more may emerge). These organizations go out into the world and track where your music is being performed publicly and, in turn, collect a performance royalty from the users. They then deliver it to the writer via a check issued either quarterly or biannually.

So what's the difference between the PROs? There are some subtle differences between all of them. Best advice, do your own research and go with the one you feel offers the most for you and the genres into which your music fits.

Know also that you can be a member of only one PRO at a time. If you sign up with one and aren't happy, you can switch to another, but watch for potential changes in income.

Signing Up (Twice)

It is critical for anyone who creates original music to sign up with a PRO as soon as possible. Not only will it collect any potential royalties, but it is also a way to register your songs and offer a second layer of protection.

Anyone is allowed to sign up to either ASCAP or BMI; however, SESAC and Global Music Rights are invitation only. ASCAP and BMI are the largest PROs in the United States. Registering with a PRO is as easy as going to their respective websites and following the sign-up instructions.

The tricky thing that most writers don't know is that you need to sign up twice: you sign up initially as an author (writer, composer) and as a *publisher*. What's the difference you ask? An author or writer means *you*—that is you as the creator, and you will need to have a personal account to represent your works. A publisher is an entity that represents *you* and controls the administrative rights to your music. Basically, without a publisher, you can't license your music; hence, you can't make money off your music. Many record labels have a publishing arm that can represent their artists, but do your homework before you sign with a publisher.

When you set up your writer account, it will be fairly straightforward. It's *you*, your name, any pseudonyms you may use as an artist, your tax ID/ social security number, address, and so on. However, when you set up your publishing, you will need to create an entity. Now, if you have already set up a DBA or an LLC to deal with these things, you could use that company's name as the publisher. Don't worry if you haven't done that yet; you can still set up your own publishing company. It's actually very similar to setting up a DBA. You will be asked to provide up to five different names to use as a publisher, and the first available one will be used.

The other purpose of having a publishing company is that they control what is known as "administrative rights" for the work. The publisher gives permission or "license" to third parties for the use of your songs in film, TV, print, and the like. If a song has multiple publishers, all the publishers will have to agree to license the song unless one publisher is given the administrative rights. They can then act on behalf of all the entities involved.

The other reason you need to register as a writer *and* a publisher is because of the way that royalties are distributed.

In order to collect any royalties, you will have to register your songs via your PRO's website. When you do this, you will enter all the pertinent information regarding the song: song title, writers, publishers, and the percentages to which the parties are entitled (otherwise known as the "splits").

If you are the sole writer of a song, you are entitled to 100% of the royalties. However, the way the royalty breaks down is 50% goes to the writer, and 50% goes to the publisher. So if you don't have a publisher, you would receive only half of your royalties. (BMI uses a 200% model, wherein the writers share gets divided from 100% of the writing, and the publisher's share is divided from 100% of the publishing—it's still the same breakdown.)

For instance, if you earn $1,000 in royalties, your PRO will divvy up the money between your writer's account and your publisher's account evenly—fifty-fifty: $500 will go to your writer and $500 to your publisher.

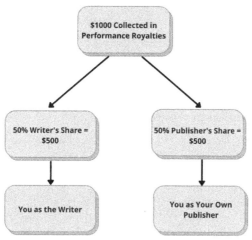

Figure 5.3. Performance Royalty Flow Chart A
Author

This is the situation if you are the only writer on the song. If you collaborate with someone else or write a song as a band, things change a bit.

For example, if your band writes a song, there are three of you, and you want to register the song with your respective PRO. Two members are ASCAP and one is BMI. The good thing is that the PROs talk to and see each other. When you sign up initially, you will receive an ID number that links to your personal information. When registering the song, only one member needs to fill in the information, and it will spread to everyone's respective accounts.

The member registering should put in everyone's ID number under the writers' and publishers' sections while registering the songs, and then their information will be populated automatically. Once everyone's personal information is entered, the last thing that needs to be done is enter the splits. This is where you determine what percentage of ownership to which each member is entitled. If you feel the drummer wasn't as influential in writing the song as the bass player, you could give them a smaller split of the song, which also means less royalty money.

Here's an example:

- Remember, a song is worth 100% (50% writers/50% publishers)
- You've decided to register the song as follows:

    Singer—55%; bassist—35%; drummer—10%; so if you add up all the percentages, you get 100%.

Here's where the math gets tricky.

- The singer owns 55% of 100%—you will need to put the splits in between the writer's share and the publisher's share as follows:
  - 55% of the 50% writer's share = 27.5% (writer's)
    - (.55 × .50 = .275 or 27.5%)
- You would do the same math for the singer's publisher share as well:
  - 55% of the 50% publisher's share = 27.5% (publisher's)
    - (.55 × .50 = .275 or 27.5%)

    The total of the singer's, writer's, and publisher's share equals 55% of the entire song.

    The bassist would be as follows—35% share.

    - .35 × .50 = .175 or 17.5%
    - 17.5% for both writer's and publisher's share for the bassist

    And finally, the drummer—10% share.

    - .10 × .50 = .05 or 5%
    - 7.5% for both the writer's and publisher's share for the drummer

When a royalty comes in for the song, it will be split between the members thusly. Using the $1,000 royalty example again, here's what everyone gets paid:

- Singer/Songwriter:
  - Writer's share is 27.5% × 1,000 = $275 in the form of a writer's check
  - Publisher's share is 27.5% × 1,000 = $275 in the form of a publisher's check
  - Grand total = $550 for the singer
- Bassist:
  - Writer's share is 17.5% × 1,000 = $175
  - Publisher's share is 17.5% × 1,000 = $175
  - Grand total = $350 for the bassist
- Drummer:
  - Writer's share 5% × 1,000 = $50
  - Publisher's share 5% × 1,000 = $50
  - Grand total = $100 for the drummer

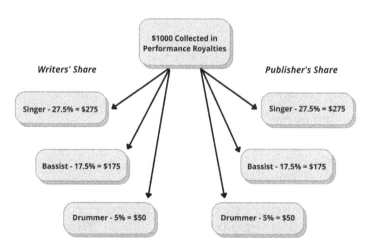

Note that the percentages from each share equal a total of 50%

Figure 5.4. Performance Royalty Flow Chart B/Multiple Writers
Author

Doing the splits can be stressful, especially when you're trying to decide who contributed more or less to a certain project. If you short someone on their contributions, you could encounter a lot of hurt feelings. Good diplomatic advice—give everyone the same splits. It makes the math easier, and no one feels slighted. (That's just my two cents.)

To get everyone on the same page as far as the splits go, it's recommended to use a *split sheet*. Here's an example of one:

SONGWRITER SPLIT SHEET

Song Title: _____

Date of Recording: _____
(If more than one day, include each day)

Recording Artist: _____ Record Label: _____

Studio Name: _____

Sample Used? Yes/No

Song and Artist Where Sample Originated: _____

Composer/Writer #1: _____

Phone #: _____ **Email:** _____

Performing Rights Organization: _____ **Writer %:** _____

Publishing Company: _____ **Publishing %:** _____

Writer/Composer Signature: _____

CAE/IPI#: _____

Composer/Writer #2: _____

Phone #: _____ **Email:** _____

Performing Rights Organization: _____ **Writer %:** _____

Publishing Company: _____ **Publishing %:** _____

Writer/Composer Signature: _____

CAE/IPI#: _____

Figure 5.5. Songwriter Split Sheet
Author

It's a good idea to have a few of these on hand whenever you're writing with others, just so there are no surprises when the first royalty checks start coming in.

One final thing: If you're working with someone who isn't signed up with a PRO yet, you can still register the songs. You can input the name of the other writer, and when it comes time to assign publishing to that writer, there is an option to leave the publisher unknown. However, they won't be able to collect any royalties until they are registered as a writer *and* a publisher. And if your song becomes a hit, trying to collect royalties after the fact is nearly impossible. So before you even start, make sure everyone is signed up.

Publishing Deals

It may seem impractical to have to split up your songs between a writer's side and a publisher's side. Remember though, publishers are the entities that give permission to use your songs; otherwise, you won't be able to make money if a third party wants to use your songs.

While you absolutely need to sign up as a self-publisher in the beginning, over time you may attract the attention of a larger publisher. They may offer you what is known as a "publishing deal."

What a publishing deal typically entails is your giving control of the publisher's share of all of your songs to a third party. This means that they will control to whom, what, and where your songs get licensed. It also means that they will collect your publisher's mechanical income check instead of you. So they may get half of your royalties (depending how you negotiate this part of the deal).

Sounds appalling, right? What do you get out of it? That depends on the quality of the deal being offered. Larger publishers will typically offer a cash advance for control of your publishing. They may offer you $25,000–$100,000 for a seven-year deal. What they don't always tell you is that if they don't recoup the advance from your publisher royalties over the next seven years, you're on the hook for the remaining balance, with interest (a lot of interest).

Still sound bad?

One other thing to understand about a publishing deal is that they don't *own* your publishing. They are renting it basically for a period of time. Many deals are about seven years, at the end of which all of your publishing reverts back to you.

Why would you ever want to sign with a publisher then? For one thing, a third-party publisher sometimes has a greater reach than you ever could because they have an established business and reputation. Large publishers like BMG or Warner-Chappell have been around for a long time, and they represent some of the largest artists. Getting a deal with one of them could open a world of opportunities for your music. The flip side to a larger company is that you may not get as much personal attention as you would at a midsized publisher. Keep those things in mind.

Also remember this, *while the publisher is collecting your publishing checks, you are still receiving your writer's check.* So if they start getting your music licensed—therefore generating more performance royalties—you get to keep half of what they get for you.

Some advice on publishing deals:

If you're ever offered one, don't just jump at it. Do some deep research on the publisher. See what they have done in the last year for their artists. Ask them point blank what you can expect from them. Is the advance recoupable? How long is the contract? All relevant and important questions to ask and never be afraid to do so.

If possible, a good entertainment attorney could help you navigate a deal so everyone walks away happy.

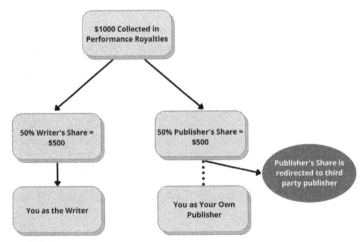

Figure 5.6. Performance Royalty Flow Chart C/Third-Party Publisher

Author

CHAPTER SIX
TYPES OF PERFORMANCE GIGS AND GIG PROTOCOLS

G one are the days in the music industry of doing just one thing and expecting that to be your career. Until you've become well known and established in one particular field, to make a decent living as a musician, you're going to have to wear several different hats. Your early career may be a mix of live performance, with a little studio work, supplemented by a bit of teaching.

This is normal, especially when you're just starting out on your journey. Over this next chapter is a list of potential gigs for you to start thinking about, along with (1) the skills necessary for them, (2) how to charge and approximately what you should be charging, and (3) ideas about where to start searching for them.

To achieve success in any of the following types of gigs, you will need to possess Three Core Skills:

- Technical proficiency

- A great ear

- The ability to communicate with others

Each gig also presents its own set of additional skills, which are addressed as you progress through them.

Create a Website

It is vital for your success as a working musician to have a website that showcases your capabilities. Before you venture off into the world of looking for work, it's a good idea to have one up and running (see Chapter 4).

Live Performance Gigs

The Solo Gig

When I say the word "solo" gig, I mean just that. These are the gigs you do on your own. If you're a pianist, guitarist, singer, or any other type of instrumentalist, you can do a solo gig. Often, these gigs require you to provide some form of "ambience" for a particular event. They're not necessarily a showcase of your talent. Think of any movie scene that has a cocktail party going on in it. There's always some light, smooth piano playing in the background, setting the tone for the party. That's essentially the gig. Every now and then, you may have a guest that takes an interest in what you're doing, but usually you're there as part of the scenery.

The only exception to this theory is if you get hired to play the ceremony at a wedding. In this situation, *everyone* is paying attention to what you're doing, so don't mess up. No pressure.

Skills Needed for Solo Gigs

- The Three Core Skills

- A vast repertoire of material based on the client's demands and enough to cover the duration of the gig

- A knowledge of current popular songs, should one be requested

- The ability to set up, maintain, and troubleshoot your own equipment

- The capability to act as an impromptu DJ, should you be required to provide music during your breaks

What's Expected of You

As stated before, these types of gigs are not concerts; they're *you* providing "ambience."

Make sure that you ask whoever hired you what style of music they want as well if there are any specific tunes that they would like you to play.

A good habit to get into with any gig is to make sure you show up early—at a minimum, one hour before you're supposed to start, or as is sometimes said, "One hour before downbeat." This way you will have plenty of time to *load-in* and set up. There's a saying that goes "If you're on time, you're late." Don't forget to account for things like traffic and parking as well. Most venues provide parking for their entertainment; however, double-check with whomever booked you before you leave for the gig.

When you arrive at the gig, there is normally a *person of contact*, or *POC*. The first thing you should do is ask where this person is and "check-in" with them. The POC is someone who either works for the venue or the agency that hired you, and *you should have a contact number for them provided to you prior to the day of the gig.*

The POC tells you where to set up and when they want you to start.

Most of these gigs will be in the two- to four-hour range, with a break every hour. Typically, 45/15 (forty-five minutes playing, fifteen-minute break), but double-check with your POC to ensure that both of you are on the same page schedule-wise.

Unless you're playing a grand piano at the venue, chances are you are going to need some sort of amplification system to be heard throughout the event. A lot of companies make portable PA systems for these types of gigs. So look into them if you plan on doing a lot of solo gigs. This is also an essential piece of equipment to incorporate any backing tracks into your performances.

Another important thing to ask is if they need you to provide music during your breaks. There's nothing worse than when you stop playing and go on break and the party has this uncomfortable silence hovering over it. Therefore, plan on providing music on your breaks, even if when you get there, they have it covered. It's better to have it and not need it than to need it and not have it.

It's also a good idea to bring a long extension cord and some duct tape (preferably black) with you to the event. Many times, I have shown up at an event, and they want me to set up in a place far away from the nearest power outlet. Trust me when I say, trying to hunt down an extension cord at the venue that's long enough can be a stressful situation. Better to have one on hand, just in case.

The attire you wear on a solo gig will be dictated by whomever hired you. Most times, you'll be requested to wear something formal. However, now and then, a party may have some sort of theme to it, be it tropical or roaring '20s. Ask ahead of time what you should wear. It's extremely embarrassing to show up in a tux to a "Jimmy Buffet–style" party.

One last piece of advice on these types of gigs would be some of the unspoken protocols that may not be written into your contract but, none-theless, you need to understand.

Unwritten Protocols

While you're on these types of gigs, there is typically no drinking or smoking of any kind. And eating is allowed only during your breaks, and that's only if your POC gives you the go-ahead to partake in the food at the event. If food is offered, make sure you go somewhere away from the guests to eat.

Where to Find Solo Gigs

Believe it or not, finding a solo gig is easier than you may think. Most upscale hotels and restaurants hire solo musicians to play their cocktail hour. If it's a restaurant, you can ask the manager if they're looking for some entertainment during their dinner rush.

Hotels, on the other hand, usually have an "event/entertainment coordinator" on-site, whose sole job is ensuring that the guests have an entertaining experience during their stay.

The entertainment coordinator assists with the planning of weddings, booking bands to play by the pool, or hiring a DJ for a corporate event that they may be hosting. All entertainment decisions go through them, and most have a list of musicians that they call upon to fulfill any needs that may arise. Your goal should be to get on that list. The hotel/resort's website should have a list of the personnel that work there, along with an appropriate email contact. Reach out to the event coordinator with a simple but direct email; it could say something like this:

Hello, my name is (blank), and I am a solo (whatever instrument you play). I am interested in offering my services to you and your organization for any future events that may require a (insert instrument here).

I have a vast repertoire of current and classic music that could make any event feel that much more special.

Here is a link to some of my work.

(Insert a web link to your online demo reel, or EPK.)

Thank you so much for your time and consideration,
(Your name)

Short and sweet.

Before you start reaching out to these potential clients, make sure that you have your website and demo reel in order.

Repeat this process with all the upscale hotels and resorts in your area. While they may not use you right away, often they will keep your information on file should one of their regular musicians not be available. If you haven't heard back from them in a couple of months, follow up with another brief email or a polite phone call to prod their memory.

Another avenue to check out when looking for solo gigs is local entertainment agencies, wedding planners, or party planners. Getting in touch with any of these entities is as easy as a quick Google search in your area. Just like the hotels, these agencies have a list of musicians that they can call upon to fulfill any of their client's demands.

Reaching out to them is no different than reaching out to the hotels. Send them a brief email letting them know you exist, with a link to your website, so they can check you out on their own time.

Some agencies may have you come in and "audition" for a spot on their roster. This is totally normal. Just make sure you have a couple of pieces prepared in different genres. You may be asked to play a straight classical piece for a wedding; then they may request something "jazzy" for the cocktail hour, and then, ultimately, something more contemporary. Therefore, it's important for you to have your musical bases covered before you walk in. The more diverse you are, the more likely it is they will hire you for a gig.

One more option for rounding up some solo gigs is to go to one of the many bridal expos that occur throughout the year. This option may cost you some money up front, but it can be worth it. Bridal expos are essentially trade shows for brides-to-be. Think National Association of Music Merchants (NAMM), but for weddings. Future brides come to these events seeking out services like photographers, caterers, florists, and entertainment.

Paying for a small booth at one of these trade shows and setting up and performing as thousands of potential gigs walk around you is an extremely effective way of marketing yourself. I've walked out of a bridal expo with between thirty and fifty bookings for the coming year.

Make sure you have either business cards, a flyer, or a brochure that they can take with them, to contact you later. If you want to take it a step further, offer a discount if they book you and put down a deposit during the expo.

No pun intended, or maybe pun intended, but you can literally "cash in" on their excitement as they daydream about their perfect wedding day.

The Pay for Solo Gigs

As far as pay goes, it most likely will be negotiated beforehand. You'll receive a standard *work-for-hire* agreement from either the venue or the agency that hired you. If you're booking your own gigs, you should provide a contract with whomever has hired you. This makes you look fancy and very businesslike.

The typical pay for a two- to four-hour solo gig can range anywhere from $200–$500. Count on at least $100 per hour minimum. Holiday parties and special events can warrant a bit more than this, but you should take it on a case-by-case basis. Don't be afraid to negotiate.

The time frame in which you're paid may take up to two weeks if you are dealing with an agency. If you booked the gig yourself, talk to your POC beforehand about who is responsible for paying you and when. Payment terms should be laid out within your contract.

Working as a Side-Person

Working as a side-person (sometimes referred to as a sideman/side-woman) can be another lucrative path for performing live. The definition of a side-person is this: *A professional musician who is hired to perform live with either a solo artist or with a group in which they are not a regular member.*

Basically, you're a hired gun. You show up, play, get paid, and go home. You're not a permanent member of the band. Therefore, you are detached from the drama that may come along with being a member.

Skills Needed as a Side-Person

- The Three Core Skills

- Versatility (you can cover a wide range of genres easily)

- Stage presence (no shoe gazing unless you're working for a shoe-gaze band)

- Adaptability

- The capacity to learn and retain an immense amount of material in a short amount of time

- The ability to make the most of your equipment and dial in the appropriate sounds for any given song

Just a quick note on learning songs for either a cover band or solo artist: If your goal is to be a professional side-person, at any level, it is imperative that you learn the songs you're given exactly as they are recorded or requested. That means playing the correct parts with the correct sounds and tones. My advice for learning material is this: learn everything in the song. If you're the guitarist, learn the bass line, keyboard part, melody, and so on. Know every song like the back of your hand. This comes in handy if the bass player's rig goes down in the middle of a song. If you know the bass line, hit your octave pedal, and you can cover for them until they're back up and running.

The thing about playing live shows is that you don't ever stop, no matter what. If a band stops in the middle of a song because of a technical problem, that's an amateur move, and the band probably won't be asked back.

You may also be called upon to learn an immense amount of material in a very short period of time, and because most groups don't use charts, you're going to have to rely on your ears to get it done. I once had to learn around thirty songs in a twenty-four-hour period. This is the reason training your ears is a core skill you need to develop. You never know when you may get called for a last-minute gig, and if you do, you'll be prepared.

Types of Side-Person Gigs

Club Gigs

A club gig is exactly what you think it is: a gig in a club. Most club gigs are cover band situations, although if an original band is good enough and they can consistently draw a crowd, they may be offered a weekly slot on a club's schedule.

Quite honestly, the club gig is about one thing—selling drinks. And you sell drinks by making people thirsty. You make people thirsty by getting them to dance. And most people only dance to songs to which they know the words. Hence, the likelihood that if you're in a club, you're playing covers.

What's Expected of You

Club gigs are pretty loose compared to most other gigs. That doesn't mean that you still don't approach them professionally.

Just like the solo gigs, plan to show up at least one hour before "downbeat." This will give you plenty of time to get everything set up, make sure your equipment is working properly, and to chill before you start playing. Try to find out beforehand where you can load-in and park so you're not driving circles around the venue wondering where to go.

As far as the attire you wear, that's really up to the band director/ music director. Some gigs may want you to look more formal; other times, they don't care what you wear. Don't be afraid to ask.

Most club gigs are pretty lax about the band having a drink or two during the night. Some even offer up drink tickets for band members. However, everything in moderation. Just because you can have a drink doesn't mean you should get soused on a gig.

Another thing that may happen during a club gig is that a patron may send the band a round of drinks; it's considered rude to turn it down. Even if you don't drink, accept it with a smile and set it somewhere out of sight, or pass it along to another band member who will happily accept it, most likely the drummer.

Typical gigs will be between three and four hours in length, with a break every hour. Remember, you'll need to add an extra hour on the front and back of these for load-in and load-out.

How to Get Involved in the Club Scene

If you're new to town or just new to the music scene in your town, one way to start getting other musicians to take note of your existence is going to your local jam sessions. There's always a good one in every town where all the "real" players go. Find out where it is and go check it out. You may want to go to a few before you offer yourself up to play. Get a feel for what the band does and what kind of tunes they play. Make some notes, go home, and woodshed those tunes.

It's important to remember that when you finally sit in, this is going to be the band's first impression of you as a player. And as they say, you never get a second chance to make a first impression. So make sure you're prepared before you jump on stage.

Another option is to find a band that's working a lot and follow them around to their gigs. Introduce yourself to the person that plays your instrument, compliment them, ask them about their gear, ask them about other gigs they're doing, and so on. (follow the script from Chapter 3 if you need help).

One thing you should never do on someone else's gig is to ask to sit in. It's rude. You want them to ask you. You can make this happen by just showing up to a bunch of their gigs, make your presence known, and most importantly, *be cool.* Eventually, you'll be thought of as that cool person who always comes out, and the band will get curious about you and most likely offer you a chance to sit in on a tune or two. Make sure you've been practicing some of the songs in their set so you don't go all "deer in the headlights" because you don't know the tune. Remember—first impressions.

For me, the most effective way of getting work as a sideman was to take lessons from someone who was already established in the scene. Most working musicians supplement their income with some teaching on the side. Find out if one of the band members offers lessons and if they do, sign up for a month or two. This is a great way to show them in a non-threatening way that you are capable of showing up on time and following directions and are technically proficient enough to get the job done.

I got my first gigs when I was around fifteen years old because my guitar teacher saw that I was extremely capable of learning things fast and playing them back correctly.

When I moved to LA, I had already been working as a professional guitarist for a number of years. The first thing I did was sign up to take some classes at the Musician's Institute, not because I couldn't play, but because I knew that most of the teachers there were working professionals and this gave me an "in" to show my value.

Within a month, I got my first gig in LA *subbing* for one of my teachers in a Top 40 band. That introduced me to the other band members, who saw that I was capable, and before I knew it, I was working three or four nights a week. And I had been in LA for only about three months at that point.

While it may cost you a little money to take the lessons, they can pay for themselves in dividends if you approach it correctly.

The Pay for Club Gigs

Depending on the size of the band, the pay for club dates can be as little as $50 a person up to $200 per person. This all depends on if the band gets a cut of the door or a percentage of alcohol sales. So count on the average pay for a club gig to hover around $100 per member.

Unlike gigs you book for yourself, you probably will not be dealing directly with the person at the venue that pays you. You'll most likely be paid by the band leader.

Sometimes, the club will pay the band with a check that the band leader will have to cash, and you will be paid at a later date. Probably, within a day or two. Often, the venue can cash the check and pay the band directly with cash, which is nice because you leave with some pocket money.

If, however, you find yourself having to constantly call a particular band director asking them to pay you for gigs that you've already played and you keep getting the runaround, have no fear: I've developed a fairly foolproof way of making sure you get paid for your club gigs. Just follow these steps:

Step 1. Don't get angry.
Step 2. Don't cancel any future gigs.
Step 3. Do show up to the next gig.

Step 4. Park all your gear on the dance floor in front of the stage.

Step 5. Wait.

Step 6. When the band leader that owes you money shows up and asks you why you're not set up, reply, very calmly, "I'll start setting up everything as soon as we take care of the pay for the previous gigs."

This is sometimes referred to as "drawing your line in the sand." I know this seems a bit passive-aggressive, and it is somewhat. However, you are honoring your word by showing up to the gig, you are willing to set up and play, but you are holding the band leader accountable to their word that they would pay you for the gigs you've already done.

Plus, because you are doing this with no time for the band leader to replace you, you put them between a rock and a hard place. You have the leverage in this situation. They need you to set up and play or else the band will look bad, and you're there ready to go.

I'll admit, I've only ever had to pull this stunt twice in my career. Both times, I was paid immediately and went on to set up and play the rest of the night. And never had an issue with getting paid again with this person. It's just business.

The other unforeseen side effect of pulling this move was that the story of my stand on the dance floor was told throughout the music scene. It became like a tall tale. People understood that you should probably pay Kris on time, or he'll pull something like this again. And I would have.

Pulling a move like this may also get you fired. Honestly, do you really want to work for someone that refuses to pay you what they've agreed?

The Casual Gig

The casual gig is the next tier of gig you will come across as a sideperson. You can think of a casual band as a high-end cover band. They tend to be more regimented and professional than your average club gig. A casual can be a wedding, corporate party, a bar or bat mitzvah, casinos, or any other event that is looking for high-end entertainment.

Because casuals tend to focus their efforts on higher-end, one-off gigs, the pay is significantly better than most club gigs.

What's Expected of You

The casual gig requires you to be exceptionally proficient on your instrument, have a good stage presence, and carry yourself with extremely professional decorum while working. Because a good casual band can demand anywhere from $5,000 on the low end, up to $20,000 for the larger events, the clients expect the band to handle themselves appropriately.

A good casual band requires rehearsals as well, and you will probably not be paid for the rehearsal time. You do, however, make up for this by making significantly more money from these gigs.

When learning the set list for a casual, another thing to take into consideration is that not only are you expected to play the parts as they are on the recording, but you also need to double-check that you are using the right sounds. Therefore, make sure you are able to recreate the sounds or tones that were used on the original recording or get as close as possible. People will notice if you're playing "Brown Eyed Girl" with a fuzz pedal. So spend some time with the original recordings and dial things in appropriately.

Whereas with a club gig, you can show up an hour before the gig starts sans issues, with a casual, you may find that you are required to show up at noon for a gig that doesn't start until 9:00 p.m. The main reason for this is that most casual events don't take place in venues that have built-in sound systems or stages, which means they have to bring in all the equipment early in the day, set it up, and make sure everything works long before the actual event starts. The band director should let you know what time they expect you to arrive.

You may also find that there is some travel involved with casuals. Most of the time, the events are within driving distance, so consider travel time and traffic. Also, make sure your vehicle is in good shape and well maintained. If you're unsure if your vehicle will make the drive, see if you can carpool with another band member. You will also be responsible for paying for your own gas and food while en route to the gig, so save your receipts.

As far as the dress code for casuals, because they are typically high-end events, you are expected to look like a high-end band. This may mean the men wear a suit and tie and the women wear an upscale cocktail dress. Or if the party is theme oriented, you may find yourself in a flowery Hawaiian shirt. Whoever booked the band will let you know the dress code.

Make sure that before you leave for the gig, you are showered and shaved and look presentable. You may not get a chance to freshen up before the show starts. Also, be sure your stage clothes are pressed and cleaned before you leave.

I advise against traveling while wearing your stage clothes. Keep them hung on a hanger and covered in a garment bag while traveling. Most casual gigs should have some form of a *green room* or space where the band can stash their equipment cases and get changed. If not, you may need to perfect the art of the "bathroom stall quick change!"

Depending on the type of casual it is, you may find that each set you play may vary. You may start with the "dinner" set and play some light jazz while people are eating. The second set may be a more oldies or adult contemporary set, so as not to scare grandma and grandpa from the venue. You'll typically end the night with the high-energy dance set, consisting of current Top 40 tunes and the classic "get everyone out of their seat and onto the dance floor tunes."

It should be written into the contract for the band how long each set is and what type of music is expected. Again, the sets shouldn't be more than an hour with a fifteen-minute break in between. Most casuals will offer a dinner break for the band, which may be thirty to forty-five minutes. If you're really lucky, they'll let you partake in the catering at the event. You should always make sure that you've been given the okay before you jump in the buffet line. Also, make sure to take your food and go away from the guests to eat.

There are certain gigs where the client doesn't want the band to partake in the food that the other guests are enjoying. If this is the case, they should have something set up with either the venue or the caterer to provide the band with a meal. This normally consists of really dry turkey sandwiches (it's always turkey sandwiches).

Drinking at casuals is typically frowned upon. You are there to provide these people with entertainment, and they're there to get loose. Not the other way around.

There are some instances where the band will be required to sign what's known as an NDA, or nondisclosure agreement. This is common when playing events with celebrities or extremely wealthy patrons. It essentially means that whatever happens at the gig, stays at the gig. This is so the guests can really let loose without the fear of having some scandalous pictures showing up on Instagram. I played an amazing event once for Patti LaBelle and Stevie Wonder, and that's all I can ever say about it.

One last thing about the casual gig: Don't fraternize with the guests. Weddings and holiday parties are fun, and you will encounter many a drunk party guest. As tempting as it may be to engage in shenanigans with a party guest, it not only makes you look bad but makes the band look bad and whoever hired the band as well.

It's okay to flirt; that's part of being an entertainer. Acting on it is a different thing altogether. If the party guest is cute, get their number, and call them when you're not working. Try to maintain your professionalism while on the gig.

Finding Casual Gigs

Getting involved in a group that plays casual gigs can be much more challenging than a group that plays standard club gigs. However, every region tends to have at least one or two bands that do most of the high-end gigs in the area. While it's almost impossible to attend their performances, because they are normally private events, you should at least find out the names of the bands getting this work and who the members are.

What will help you the most is getting the players in your area to see you as reliable, professional, and technically proficient enough to handle a more high-pressure situation. It may take some time to develop this type of reputation, but you can start by approaching every gig you do, even the small ones, with the utmost professionalism.

One tip to help speed along the process would be to put a microphone in front of you on all of your gigs. Even if you're not a great singer, casual bands love musicians that can also sing background vocals.

Take a vocal lesson and have the teacher show you how to breathe properly and hold a note. The minute I started doing this on my gigs, I was immediately offered more high-paying situations. I'll admit that I can't carry a tune by myself, but I can hold a note if you tell me what note to sing.

The Pay for Casual Gigs

A good casual band can demand far more money than an average club band. Therefore, it's not unheard of for each musician to walk away with between $200 and $500 per show. Holiday parties and special events can demand more, especially New Year's Eve gigs. It's not unheard of for each musician to make as much as $1,000 for a New Year's gig with a good band.

Backing Up an Artist

When most people think of a "hired gun" or side-person gig, the one that probably comes to mind would be backing up a solo artist. These are the types of gigs where you play the artist's original music. Think of these gigs in three different levels: the local artist, the mid-level artist, and the international (signed) artist.

The skills required for these gigs are the same as any other side-person gig, with varying degrees of expertise. The job itself is the same for all three—you are there to make the artist look and sound good.

The Local Artist

Sometimes referred to as an *indie* or independent artist is the artist who is just emerging in the scene with their original music. They tend to have very little, if any, financial backing, no management, and a small to medium draw of fans, most likely consisting of friends and family.

What's Expected of You

The local independent artist may have just finished an *EP* (extended play) recording with four or five songs that they are trying to promote. Your job is to learn those songs and recreate them as closely as possible to the recordings.

Unless you're in one of the music meccas like Nashville or Los Angeles, there generally aren't many venues that cater to original music. This will obviously impact the number of gigs that are available to the artist. Even when you do find a venue that caters to original music, unless the artist has a massive draw of fans, the pay can be negligible. This is true even in the larger music cities.

This doesn't mean that these gigs aren't worth doing. Backing up an indie artist can be a lot of fun, and it's great for building your experience of working as a side-person. Just don't expect to make a lot of money in these situations.

This is a prime example of the "unless you want to" part of the rule in Chapter 1. A good friend of mine said this to me once: "There are three things I look for on a gig—good music, good people, or good money. If a gig hits two out of three, I'll do it." Next time you're on the fence about taking a gig, hold it up to this list. See if it's a good fit or not.

Finding These Gigs

If you want to start finding work with independent artists, you need to go to the places where they are. Find the venues in your area that cater to original music and start frequenting them.

I got one of my first gigs backing up an indie artist in LA by going to a songwriter showcase at a venue called The Mint. One artist in particular caught my attention. A piano-playing singer/songwriter who didn't have a band backing her up, but she had some really lovely songs. I took note of her name, found her artist page via social media, and sent her a message that went something like this: "Hi, my name is Kris and I saw your performance at The Mint this evening. I'm a guitarist who's new to town and would like to get together and play sometime."

Somewhat like the equivalent of a cold call in sales. To my surprise, she responded immediately and told me she was looking for a guitarist with whom to work. We set up a time to meet for lunch and a little jam session.

I ended up working with her for a number of years. The gigs didn't pay much, but through her I met a lot of other artists and musicians that were working the original scene, which led to more opportunities and even a few tours.

The Pay for These Gigs

Don't expect to get rich backing up an independent artist. While the pay isn't great, you do get the opportunity to develop the skillset necessary to grow and evolve as a player.

On average, you can expect around $50–$75 a night with an indie artist. Sometimes, they can only offer you gas money. It's up to you to decide if it's something worth doing.

One thing that has happened for me while working with an indie artist is that they get offered either a publishing deal or a record deal. And if you've been a loyal part of their journey, they may take you along for the ride. Don't count on this though. Management may decide that the band needs a complete overhaul, and everyone gets let go and replaced. Unless you have a contract with the artist (which rarely happens) keep this in the back of your mind.

The Mid-Level Artist

The next level in backing up an artist is the mid-level artist. They are the artists that have some form of financial backing and/or a management team involved.

These artists fit most comfortably into the local club circuits as well as joining in some regional touring and possible *fly dates* (more on this later) to promote either an album or a single that may be getting some traction on the charts.

The mid-level artist is usually more polished and will have a fairly clear direction as far as who they are and how they want to be perceived. You'll find them in any of the major music hubs as well as some of the medium ones like Austin, Miami, Atlanta, or Portland.

What's Expected of You

The expectations of working with a mid-level artist are similar to the indie artist's but with the added pressure of management being involved. You'll need to be consistent with your performances; mistakes aren't tolerated for very long. While on stage, you also need to dress, act, and perform like you are a natural fit for the artist, or you will be replaced. It's a sad fact, but as a side-person, you are expendable. It's all about the artist. So don't give management an excuse to replace you.

Finding These Gigs

Getting involved with a mid-level artist definitely falls into a "who you know" situation. If you've been playing with the artist since their indie days, then you have a leg up on most other musicians. However, it's still not a guarantee that they'll keep you on board once their career starts to take off.

Usually, these gigs will come about based on a recommendation. Perhaps you played a different gig with the bass player, and they recommended you for this one. Even though you may come recommended, you'll probably still have to audition. Management and label execs are very concerned with how their artists are presented, so they may be involved in the audition process as well.

The Pay for These Gigs

The pay you can expect working with a mid-level artist can range from $150 per show up to around $300. If you're doing some regional touring or fly dates, you can make upward of $1,500 per week, plus travel expenses. The pay you receive is ultimately determined by the amount of financial backing or tour support to which the artist has access.

The Audition

If there was one thing that I wish someone would have explained to me before I moved to LA, it would have been how to properly do a "real" audition.

My first real audition in LA was for a mid-level rock band. They were signed to a label, had tour support, and were booked on all the late-night shows, and the label was about to do a big marketing push to get them some more airplay on the radio.

The pay wasn't the best, but it was steady: $1,000/week plus a per diem when traveling.

Having only ever done my audition to get into college, I figured that all I needed to do to get the gig was nail the songs and look presentable. So I put on a cool button-down shirt and wore some flared slacks and square-toed, shiny black shoes. Something I would wear on a high-end casual. I felt self-assured.

This was a *cattle call* audition, where the label puts out the word publicly and hundreds of players show up. I felt I looked more presentable than the hundred other guitarists that showed up and was feeling very confident.

My confidence was immediately crushed the second I walked into the room. And I realized that I'd already messed the whole thing up before I even played a note. The band members were standing around in ripped-up jeans and T-shirts, and I looked like I was about to play a wedding. "Okay, okay, I just need to play great, and they'll see past it," I said to myself.

I proceeded to absolutely nail every song, played some ripping solos, had the guys in the band egging me on. I thought "phew, I saved it." The MD (music director) of the band came over, slapped my back, and asked me when I could start. I was stoked!

They asked me to wait outside while they went through the rest of the guitarists. It was just a "formality" is what they told me; I had the gig.

At the end of the audition, they called me back in and management was standing there. The band was explaining that I was the "guy"; however, management disagreed. The manager pointed out the way I was dressed and said I wasn't a good fit. I told him that he could just tell me what to wear and I would do it. Then he said the thing that sealed my fate, "but he doesn't even have any tattoos."

I learned a very important lesson that day about going on auditions. While it's absolutely important that you are able to play what's required of you on your instrument, almost as equally important is how you present yourself. My advice for auditions is this:

- Learn and play the parts exactly as they are on the recordings given to you; that means dialing in the correct sounds too.

- Do some research on the artist's aesthetic and show up looking like you could just hop on stage and you belong there.

- Be prepared to show off a bit; this doesn't happen often, but they may throw you a curve ball.

- Be cool. Nobody wants to be stuck on a bus with an insufferable twit.

International Artist

To many players, this is the ultimate gig: Backing up a named international artist. These gigs require you to be at the top of your game.

These are the artists who are signed, have massive tour and label support, and most likely have a hit song or two on the charts.

Because these gigs are so high-profile, there is very little to no room for error at any given point. You may be playing to a crowd of 50,000 fans on an arena tour, or millions of viewers via a late-night show. One mistake and it can all be over.

These gigs will most likely require extensive amounts of travel and time dedication. The trade off for this commitment is the pay. By far, playing for an internationally known artist will pay you more than most any other live playing situation.

What's Expected of You

As just noted, these gigs require you to be at the top of your game both musically and mentally. Some artists are extremely affable and enormous fun to play with and be around, while others can make you feel as though you're a peasant working for a tyrant king. It really depends on the artist and how they want the show to be run.

Regardless of how the artist treats the musicians, you are expected to perform at 110% on every show. That means you play your parts right and "put on a show." Putting on a show can mean different things for different artists, but essentially it boils down to looking like you're having the time of your life while playing.

Rehearsals also become a regular part of your life on these gigs. The good news is that you will most definitely be paid for your rehearsal time.

You are also expected to carry yourself in a manner that befits the artist at all times both on- and offstage.

When you are hired for a gig like this, expect to sign some form of an NDA. Celebrities are very cautious about the personal information that gets leaked about them, so don't be surprised when one gets shoved in your face.

One final tip: If you're working with a signed international artist and a problem arises, whatever you do, don't bring it to the attention of the artist. There is a hierarchy associated with these gigs that goes something like this:

The Artist

▼

Management/Label

▼

Tour Manager

▼

Music Director

You

The music director is most likely to be your point of contact for any issues you may have. They will relay the information to the appropriate person.

Finding These Gigs

Getting involved with an international artist is an imprecise process that gets shrouded in a lot of secrecy. In reality, most artists find their musicians through auditions. However, these auditions are never widely publicized, so you have to be in the loop as to who's looking for a new band and when they may be holding auditions. You get in the loop by developing a solid reputation with the musicians in your musical community.

Every so often, an artist might do a cattle call audition. A cattle call can be chaos. Because the audition is public knowledge, hundreds or even thousands of musicians may show up.

In the 1990s, the Red Hot Chili Peppers were looking for a new guitarist, so they put out a cattle call and nearly *4,000* guitarists showed up! I'm not saying that public cattle calls don't happen anymore, but they are rare these days.

In LA, New York, and Nashville, there are what's known as *tour wranglers*. These are individuals that work directly with artists or management companies to find players for upcoming tours and will probably be the ones organizing the auditions. If you want to work these types of gigs, getting on their list should be a priority for you. Of course, this is a challenging task; it's another "who you know" situation. It may take some time and effort to prove to the musicians in your community that you are "worthy" of such an honor. You never know who you may be on a gig with, so it's important that you treat every situation like you're auditioning for your favorite artist.

I got my first opportunity from a keyboard player on a small, no money, club gig. It just so happened that he was the music director for some touring artists; he liked the way I played as well as how I carried myself. Next thing I know, I was auditioning for a well-known hip-hop group and touring across the country.

The Pay for These Gigs

Backing up an international artist is both high profile and high pressure. The pay you receive should reflect that.

Plan on $300–$500 for one-off shows. Touring should start at no less than $1,500 per week, plus per diem and travel expenses.

Usually, you will be paid by the management company on a weekly or biweekly basis. You should set up some form of direct deposit. It's advisable to do this; you don't want to be stuck in the middle of nowhere with a paper check that you can't cash or deposit.

Some payrolls are handled like any other business, where taxes are deducted before you receive your check. For others, you may be responsible for taking care of the taxes yourself. If this is the case, try to stash at least 30% of your earnings for taxes later.

LIVE PLAYING CHECKLIST

Gig Information

Band/Artist: _____

Venue: _____Address: _____

Person of Contact: _____Contact Info: _____

Band Leader/MD: _____Contact Info: _____

Start/End Time: _____Set Length/Breaks: _____

Load-in Time: _____

Load-in Location: _____Setup Location: _____

Parking: _____

Pay: _____

Gig Checklist

☐ Instrument   ☐ Amplification   ☐ Microphones

☐ Microphone Stand   ☐ Cables   ☐ Cable Ties

☐ Power and Extension cords ☐ Duct Tape   ☐ Backing Tracks?

☐ Break Music?   ☐ Stage Clothing   ☐ Food Provided?

☐ Additional Accessories (cables, batteries, picks, strings, etc.)

Additional Information or Requests

_____

_____

_____

Figure 6.1.   Live Playing Checklist
Author

Touring

If I could think of a saying that encompasses what touring is like, it would be this: *"Hurry up and wait."* While often portrayed as a glamorous life-style in film and television, the reality of life on the road isn't always as sexy as it's made out to be. This is not to say that some of the things portrayed don't happen; it's just that there can be long stretches of boredom between the excitement.

Touring is an essential part of any artist's career. The point of the tour is to get an artist in front of as many new faces as possible. This, in turn, results in more visibility, more streams, more placement opportunities, and therefore, more money.

Remember, this is the music "business." And like any good business, it's all about making a profit.

Your touring experience can vary depending on the type of artist with whom you are traveling. The "indie" or mid-level artist may see you traveling within a certain region, playing clubs, small venues, or music festivals. While with more known acts, you may be traveling nationally or internationally playing larger theaters or even stadiums.

No matter the type of tour on which you end up, there are some things to take into consideration before you leave. You may be gone for months at a time, so a little forethought can save you a lot of headaches once you're out on the road.

Per Diem

While on tour, all of your travel and accommodation expenses should be covered by either the management or the artist. This doesn't always include things like lunch or dinner. For that, along with your regular pay, you should receive what's known as a *per diem* (per day). A per diem is a daily allowance for things like food or any other daily incidental costs you may incur.

You may receive anywhere from $25 per day, up to $75, depending on the tour budget. Before you go on the road, always ask if there is a per diem. Otherwise, you will be paying out of pocket for your daily expenses. This can chew into your overall earnings from the tour, so keep this in mind.

If you're really savvy, you can learn how to eat on the cheap (but try to eat healthily) and pocket the leftover per diem as extra pay.

Prepping for a Tour

It goes without saying that you need to make sure that you have everything you will need to live out of a suitcase for the foreseeable future. That means things like clothes, hygiene products, medications, passports and identification, personal entertainment, and of course, your equipment.

Clothing

Before you head out, make sure to check the weather reports in the areas that you are traveling to. While it may be sunny and seventy degrees in LA, it could be minus fifteen in Minneapolis. I use this example because I made this mistake and I was absolutely miserable.

You'll be bringing an assortment of "stage" clothes to perform in as well as your regular daily choices. Make sure that your travel clothes are comfortable; you may be in a van for thirteen hours straight or have to wait overnight in the terminal of an airport.

Last clothing tip: Wear comfortable shoes, the best you can afford. I can't stress this enough. While touring, you may find yourself standing around for hours waiting to play. You'll want shoes that don't kill your back.

Hygiene Products

As far as personal hygiene products go, it's not a bad idea to carry extras of things like deodorant, toothpaste, floss, tampons, and the like. You may run out and there's not always a drugstore nearby to reup on these things. For shampoos and other bath products, if you're flying, remember the TSA guidelines about liquids. Best to stash these things in your checked luggage in a sealed baggie to avoid any issues.

Medications

If you require any form of necessary daily prescription medications, make sure to refill your prescriptions before you leave. Also, if you are traveling internationally, verify what can and can't be brought into a foreign country. Some places have very strict regulations about the types of medications you can carry through customs, so sort these things out well before you leave.

Don't forget to bring along things like ibuprofen for headaches, immune boosting vitamins or Airborne so you don't catch a cold, masks, antacids, or things that may help you sleep like herbal sleep aids or over-the-counter aids like Tylenol PM.

You should also make management or other bandmates aware if you have any type of deadly allergies that may require the use of an EpiPen or if you are diabetic and require regular insulin shots. It could save your life!

Passports and ID

Double-check that all of your personal identification documents are current and up to date. This means your photo ID (driver's license or other government-issued ID) as well as your passport. If your passport is about to expire, it may be a good idea to renew it before you leave. Keep these documents in a secure place where you will have easy access to them should you be asked to provide them.

If you are traveling internationally, most likely you'll need a visa of some type. Luckily, management will (hopefully) have this taken care of prior to your departure. But it's never a bad idea to double-check that everything is covered.

Losing or misplacing a passport overseas is a nightmare you don't want to have happen. There are many secure cases and travel wallets that can keep all your documents safe and secure while traveling abroad. For peace of mind, it may be worth investing in something like this.

Personal Entertainment

There can be a lot of downtime while on tour. Whether it's traveling to the next location or waiting around for a sound check. Make sure to bring something that will help pass the time.

If you like reading books, invest in a Kindle or tablet that can hold thousands of books without the weight.

You like watching movies? Wi-Fi can be spotty in some places, so don't be overly reliant on your Netflix account to work while traveling. One thing you can do is invest in a small external hard drive for either your laptop or tablet. Then you can download as many movies or TV shows it can hold and have your own personal streaming service. You can do the same if you like playing video games as well.

Make sure to bring the proper power adapters for all of your electronic devices. Perhaps even invest in a remote charge pack in case you end up not being around a power source for many hours.

If traveling internationally, buy yourself a universal power adapter. Different countries have different outlets and voltage requirements. It's advisable to purchase one of these before you leave; they'll be easier to find and cheaper than trying to get one overseas.

One more thing: Make certain that you either turn off the data roaming on your phone or purchase a sim card for whatever country you may be in. Many a musician has come home from tour with a $15,000 phone bill!

Taking Care of Your Bills While You're Away

Depending on how long you will be out on the road, you may need to come up with a solution to pay your bills while traveling. Just because you're not at home, doesn't mean the bills stop coming in.

Plan to take care of any rent or mortgage payments. If you're renting, see if you can set up an autopay with your landlord. If this isn't an option and you are required to hand over a physical check every month, write out your rent checks in advance, postdate them according to the month that they're due, and give them to your landlord before you leave. You should photocopy or scan them, too, as proof that you've already handed them out.

For all other expenses like utilities, car payments, and insurance, set up an autopay system if you haven't already. Cancel any services you may not need while out on the road to save some extra money (think streaming services). When you need them, you can always turn them back on when you get back.

Traveling with Your Equipment

Getting your gear in order before setting out on tour is a must. You should have extra everything—strings, picks, cables, reeds, rosin, batteries, tubes—anything that could break, get lost, or need to be replaced. Have backups for the backups. If you are traveling internationally, make sure that you have a step-up or step-down box to account for the different voltages used in various countries.

Have your instruments serviced to make sure they're in prime working order. Check cases for any damage and reinforce them if you are traveling by plane.

You'll probably be bringing your own instruments when you tour, especially guitar and bass. And depending on the size and scope of the tour, getting your gear to its destination safely and in working order poses a challenge.

Larger tours will have the cartage figured out. And you will probably have a tech that handles all of the logistics of moving your equipment from place to place. These techs are also known as the beloved roadies. They will ensure that your equipment is packed away correctly and arrives safe and sound, ready to go at the next venue.

However, on smaller tours, you will likely be responsible for making sure your equipment arrives safely. If you are traveling by van or bus, typically your equipment is stowed in either the back of the van or underneath the bus. Sometimes, there may be an equipment trailer being towed that will hold everything. Just be aware that a trailer sitting in the sun all day will cook your gear, so take it out when not moving. This is a relatively safe way of transporting your equipment; as long as you have some sturdy road cases, you should be fine. Always check that there is insurance on the van, bus, or trailer that covers damage and theft.

Traveling with your gear gets more complicated when you are flying to most of your shows. Since 9/11, it's become increasingly harder to travel with gear on a plane. Baggage handlers tend to not care if your cases are marked "fragile" or not. And it can be a nerve-racking experience watching them throw your beloved equipment onto the conveyor belt from the window of the plane.

For guitars and basses, you may be able to schmooze the agent at the gate and get them to allow you to board the flight early so you can grab an overhead compartment. Just be very, very, very, nice to them. On most planes, there is also a small closet near the front where the crew puts their luggage and personal items. This can be an option, as well, should all the overhead bins be full. Again, be nice when you ask. If all else fails, you may end up having to gate check your instrument. This is only slightly better than checking your instruments with your luggage, but the upside is, your instrument will likely be the last thing loaded and the first thing unloaded.

The best advice would be to invest in a TSA-approved flight case. They can be expensive, and if it weighs more than fifty pounds, you will be charged extra for checking it. But it offers the best protection while flying.

Most gigs that require you to fly provide what's known as *backline*. Backline is gear that is rented ahead of time in the city to which you are traveling, typically, drums, amps, and keyboards. More often than not, you will be asked what kind of backline you want, and you can choose the type of amp or drum kit you would like provided when you arrive. It's a nice little perk and is much cheaper to rent the equipment than to pay to have yours flown to the venue.

Most guitarists and bassists bring their own instruments and pedals, then use the provided backline for amplification. Drummers may bring their own snare, cymbals, and pedals. Keyboardists may have all of their sounds loaded onto a laptop and use whatever is provided at the venue as a MIDI controller.

Be sure to loosen the tension on stringed instruments and drumheads before you fly. The shift in air pressure can wreak havoc on the wood or heads of your instrument.

One last thing to consider when traveling with your gear is changes in climate. If you live in a dry area and travel to someplace humid, the wood in your instrument will take on moisture and therefore start to either expand or contract. This will require you to check your instruments' setup when you arrive. You may have to adjust your intonation to make sure everything plays in tune by showtime.

While on the Road

Traveling by Van or Bus

Your first tours will probably be traveling by either van or bus, depending on the level of the artist and the money backing them.

If you're lucky, a bus will be provided with bunks, meal prep area, lounge, and a bathroom. Even though there is a bathroom on the bus, the unwritten rule is "number one only!" For the sake of your traveling companions, you should abide by this. (Plus, *never* flush any sanitary products in the bus toilet. To dispose of them, carry sealable separate bags and toss them at the next stop.)

The other form of tour transport would be the van. If you've never had the joy of being stuffed in an Econoline van with ten other people, you're truly missing out on the touring experience.

In recent years in lieu of the traditional Econoline van, many smaller acts have started renting Sprinter vans, which are larger and more comfortable. Some even have Wi-Fi built in!

Whatever the mode of transportation, traveling via road can be brutal. Depending on the scope of the tour, you may spend anywhere between five and ten hours at a time driving to the next venue. And because money may be tight with the tour, there may not be a hotel provided at every stop you make.

You could show up at the venue at 2:00 in the afternoon but may not be able to load-in until 7:00 for a show that starts at 11:00. After the show, you may have to pack up everything, climb in the van, and start driving to the next destination ten hours away.

To me, this was the roughest aspect of touring; this is "hurry up and wait."

With no hotel accommodations, you are unable to shower or clean up before or after the gig. If you've ever been on a family road trip during the summer and remember how gross you felt or the smell of the car after driving all day in the hot sun, it's like that but worse.

While on the road, if you find yourself in this type of situation, try to keep a fresh, clean shirt handy to change into, brush your teeth when you have the opportunity, and learn the art of the "spit bath" (washing up in a sink). Having some baby wipes to clean the funk from more sensitive areas is an option as well. These few things can help you get through those long stints without a hotel.

Fly Dates

Fly dates are either one-off gigs or a short run of shows that are too far to drive to. Typically, acts with more financial backing do these types of gigs. You may find yourself flying to five or six different cities within the span of a week.

Traveling for a fly date is much easier than going by bus or van. Backline is normally provided, so all you are required to bring is yourself and your instrument.

Fly dates tend to always offer accommodations in the city to which you are traveling.

Be sure to ask your music director or tour manager if you are required to pay for your checked luggage. At $35 per bag (instruments too) and five or six flights per week, that is a minimum of $175 dollars you're spending out of your own pocket. Normally these fees are taken care of by the management, but in the rare occurrence that you are required to pay for your own checked bags, keep the receipt for tax purposes later.

Another thing to consider is keeping your immune system up and running while traveling by plane. Take some vitamin C or a product like Airborne before you board. Plus, what we've learned from the pandemic—bring a mask as well. There is no worse feeling in the world than having to put on a show while you have a 101 degree fever.

Having done so many fly dates in my career, I ended up building what's known as a *fly rig*. It's everything I need gear-wise, just made smaller so I can carry my guitar and pedals in the same bag. If you find yourself traveling often by plane, you may want to look into ways to pare down your equipment while still getting the sounds you need for the gig.

One final tip for fly dates (I learned this one from a tour mate) is to sign up for the rewards programs of whatever airline you are flying on. Even though you didn't pay for the tickets yourself, you can still collect the airline miles for your travels. Eventually, if you travel enough, you'll accrue enough miles for things like free tickets or even first-class upgrades! So don't sleep on this.

Accommodations

While out on the road, you'll likely be staying in a lot of hotels. If you're really lucky, you'll get your own room at every stop. Otherwise, you'll be sharing with at least one other band member.

When you check in, make sure you are carrying a credit card, not a debit card. While you may not be paying for the room, most hotels require the occupant of the room to provide a credit card for any incidentals. This would cover things like room service, drinks, or the dreaded mini bar. If you give the hotel a debit card, they may put as much as a $300 hold on it, tying up your cash. It may also take a number of days for the money to be put back on your card, making your cash reserves tighter than necessary.

Providing an actual credit card is much easier, and the hold normally disappears within twenty-four hours of checkout. If you don't have a credit card, investigate getting a prepaid one (see Chapter 9).

Getting a Good Night's Sleep

Staying well rested is vital for your health while on tour, so bring everything you may need to get a good night's sleep.

If you're a light sleeper, having a roommate on the road can be a pain. Bring some earplugs in case you get stuck with someone who snores, and bring an eye mask to keep out any extraneous light.

If you're staying in an older-style hotel/motel, most will have some form of wall unit air conditioner. My advice is to grab the bed farthest from it. Wall unit air conditioners are rarely cleaned, and they pump out some pretty low-quality air. I got the worst cold of my life in the middle of the summer in New York City because my roommate decided to put the wall AC on full blast while we slept. So be aware of your proximity to those machines.

Incidentals

Hotel incidentals are things like room service, movie rentals, or laundry services.

Beware of the mini bar and snacks placed around the room. These days, everything is connected to a sensor, so if you just pick something up or move it, you may be charged for it—ever pay $7 for a Snickers bar?

Even if you didn't use the thing that you picked up or moved, trying to get the charge reversed is difficult to say the least. Some places are cool with it, while others just want to charge you for as many things as possible. (Vegas, I'm looking at you.) My best advice is to just not touch or move anything the hotel has left out that looks too enticing. That's how they get you.

A lot of hotels will offer some sort of free breakfast for their guests. Some hotels' idea of "breakfast" is a stale muffin and burned coffee. Others may offer a really good breakfast spread. It's worth waking up a little early to check it out and maybe grab something before you head out for the day. It's a "free" meal, so that means you're not spending your per diem, which means you can pocket it for later.

Laundry

Keeping your clothes clean is an essential part of being comfortable while on tour. Luckily, most places you stay will offer some sort of laundry service or have washing machines on-site. This can be a godsend if you've been out for more than a week and are down to your last pair of socks. Having fresh clothes is like recharging the battery.

You'll most likely have to take care of the cost of laundry yourself. I've been in very few situations that covered these things.

If there is no on-site laundry, there will most likely be a laundromat near the hotel. But before you head out to wash your clothes, do a bit of research on the area you're staying in. You may be smack dab in the "bad" part of town.

I made this mistake in Detroit.

We were staying downtown, and I'd never been there. I needed to do some laundry, found the closest laundromat, and headed off.

I literally took one step off the hotel property and was surrounded by about ten people asking me for change or if I was from "around here." I promptly returned to the hotel and proceeded to wash all of my socks and underwear in the bathroom sink and put them on clothes hangers to dry (that's a tip from my lovely friend/editor Ronny Schiff).

Lobby Call

Lobby call is the time everyone is meant to be up and ready to go. If you're leaving for another city, pack everything the night before. Make sure you have all of your personal items as well as things like chargers and power cables. Doing the mad dash at 6:00 a.m. is not fun.

I usually will set at least two alarms and also have the front desk give me a wake-up call, just to make sure I'm up and out on time.

While on tour in Japan, our drummer overslept and missed lobby call and, therefore, the bus to the bullet train station. I learned that day that the people in Japan are very serious about time. If the bus leaves at 7:00, the bus leaves at 7:00!

Our drummer came running out of the hotel screaming, "Wait, wait!!!" The bus driver looked at him, shut the door, and left him there.

He ended up having to take a very expensive cab ride to the train station, which he had to pay for. Moral of the story: Don't miss lobby call.

Food

Food is another hugely important aspect of staying healthy on the road. You will probably be responsible for feeding yourself while on tour. This is what your per diem is for.

While breakfast and lunch are almost always your responsibility, some venues or shows may offer a meal, or even better, be catered! Often, you won't know for sure until you show up at sound check. If you're not certain what the food situation is, ask the tour manager, but don't make it a habit.

Another thing to consider while you're out is any dietary restrictions you may have. If you're vegan or vegetarian, you may run into some issues. Major cities won't be a problem, but when you're out in the middle of the country and ask for a vegan option, you may get a funny look.

If you have food allergies, you need to be extra cautious of where and what you eat while traveling. Even the most rural of places may have a chain you're familiar with. So better to play it safe than be sorry.

For those with no restrictions, touring can be a whole new food adventure! From Alabama BBQ, to fresh-caught salmon in the Pacific Northwest, to a slice of real New York City pizza—there's so much good food to encounter.

Try to eat as healthy as possible. There will, however, be those times when the only thing available is a gas station hot dog. Strive to counteract the bad road food with more healthy options when possible. Buy bags of nuts, or find an apple or a banana. Not only will this be good for your overall health, but you also won't come home with an extra twenty pounds.

If you're traveling through foreign countries, for the adventurous eater, it can be amazing! If you're a picky eater, it could be somewhat miserable. The good news for those that are picky is that most of the world has adopted some form of cuisine that will be familiar to you.

Do some research before you leave to find out what kind of food will be available. This will save you the headache of trying to figure out what to eat while traveling.

My advice, if you're able, is be adventurous when traveling abroad. You may not be back anytime soon, so take advantage of the situation.

New Places

While on tour, you'll mostly be traveling to places you've never been. This for me was always my favorite part of touring. It's almost like a paid sightseeing vacation.

Sometimes, the schedule won't allow you to venture out in these new places. But if and when you do get a day off or are playing multiple dates in the same place, set some time aside to explore. See if you can get some other bandmates to join the adventure with you.

Most places will have some sort of historical or cultural significance. Again, before you leave, do some research on the places you'll be traveling through. That way you will have a game plan when you've finally got a day off.

Try not to get lost though. Thankfully, with GPS in our phones, this happens less often than it used to. But do try to at least get your bearings and remember things like the name of the hotel or the venue you're playing at, just in case.

If you're traveling in the states, you'll probably have a pretty good idea of how to behave while visiting new places. When you go abroad is where you need to understand the culture and decorum that's expected of you.

Europe is fairly similar to the United States as far as the culture. Asian, African, and Middle Eastern countries are where things can be very different.

I really can't stress enough how important it is to spend time researching the places you'll be going. Some countries have very strict laws about smoking, drinking, and even chewing gum. In Singapore, you can be thrown in jail for littering! It's better to understand these things beforehand, rather than learn them the hard way.

One way to sum up traveling to a foreign country—don't be an asshole. There is that "big, dumb American" stereotype in many foreign countries, and for good reason. So don't be that person.

TOURING CHECKLIST

Tour Information

Artist: _____

Destination(s): _____

Weekly Salary: _____ Per Diem: _____

Management: _____ Contact Info: _____

Music Director: _____ Contact Info: _____

Pre-Tour Checklist

☐ Photo ID   ☐ Passport   ☐ Stage Clothing

☐ Weather-Appropriate   ☐ Personal Hygiene Products   ☐ Medications
   Clothes
                                    ☐ Chargers and Adapters   ☐ Autopay Enabled

☐ Personal Entertainment
                                      ☐ Backline Provided?   ☐ Credit Cards

☐ Instruments and Gear

Departure/Return Information

Departure Date: _____ Departure Time: _____

Departure Location: _____ Address: _____

Return Date: _____ Return Time: _____

Return Location: _____ Address: _____

Flight Information

Airline: _____ Flight Number: _____

Checked Bags: _____Yes/No_____ Frequent Flyer #: _____

Accommodations

Hotel Name: _____ Hotel City: _____

Incidentals: _____Yes/No_____ Laundry Service: _____Yes/No_____

Figure 6.2. Touring Checklist
Author

Studio Gigs—Engineering

The advancement in home studio technology has evolved at an exponential rate over the last twenty years. Because of this, to work as an engineer or producer these days requires a computer, an interface, some plug-ins, and a good ear.

The larger studios still exist to some extent, especially to do film scoring with large groups of musicians, but their numbers are diminishing.

In the early 2000s, a four-song EP would cost you around $10,000 to finish in a moderately equipped studio. These days, $10,000 can get you a powerful computer, a great interface, and all the plug-ins your heart desires, and you can make your EP, with no restrictions on time or money, from the comfort of your own home.

Because the technology has evolved, so has the way one approaches "studio work."

What You'll Need

Aside from the Three Core Skills discussed in chapter 3 (technical proficiency, a great ear, and the ability to communicate effectively), you'll need a few more elements to make yourself competitive in the studio world:

- *Computer*: Most likely a Mac (sorry PC people). Make sure it has a fast multicore processor. Max out the RAM if possible. Most applications will require at least 16GB to work their best.

- *Interface*: This is the device that will convert analog information into digital information. Typically, the more expensive, the better the conversion. The good news is that there are some excellent options on the market these days that won't break the bank. Companies like Universal Audio and Apogee offer some fantastic entry-level options. Keep in mind that the technology moves and changes quickly, so stay up to date on the latest and greatest.

- *DAW (digital audio workstation)*: This is the software you will use to record, edit, and mix the audio brought into your computer. The big three are Pro Tools (more on this one later),

Logic Pro, and Ableton Live. Find a DAW that suits your needs and your wallet.

- *Basic understanding of audio*: This should go without saying, but if you're going to work in the field of audio manipulation, you need to develop a firm understanding of how sound works. There are schools dedicated solely for this purpose if you have the time. There is also a wealth of information in the form of online tutorials and books that can get you started.

The Pro Tools Elephant in the Room

While you are free to pick and choose any DAW you like to get started, if you want to work at the highest levels of the industry, you will need to learn how to use Avid's Pro Tools.

Every major studio, postproduction facility, and film production company uses Pro Tools. It's what's referred to as "industry standard."

Pro Tools has become the universal final landing place for all high-end audio projects. So at some point, whether you like it or not, you're going to run into it. Even having a basic understanding of how Pro Tools works will be extremely beneficial.

Personally, I use Logic Pro for most of my work these days. However, I always end up exporting all of my projects to Pro Tools when I deliver them.

My best advice would be this: Learn at least two DAWs. One of your choice with which you're comfortable working *and* Pro Tools.

Engineering Gigs

An engineer's primary job is to capture and manipulate audio. It's very technically demanding work. However, there is also a creative aspect to being a good engineer as well.

One of the most creative areas of audio engineering is "mixing" all of the audio elements together to bring a sense of balance and clarity. You'll be bringing everything together as one cohesive unit in the mix.

The best way to start developing the skills needed to be an engineer is to get busy recording and editing as many projects as possible. Learning it from a purely theoretical approach can be helpful, but getting your hands dirty is the fastest way to enhance those skills.

Skills Required

- The Three Core Skills
  - Technical proficiency
  - A great ear
  - The ability to communicate with others
- An understanding of audio fundamentals
- Knowledge of various recording techniques and equipment
- Understanding various audio processors (plug-ins and hardware) and their functions
- The ability to manipulate and shape recorded audio to fit your client's demands (tuning software, time manipulation, or noise removal)
- Signal flow—The ability to route audio through busses, sends, returns, effects, and so on.
- A fundamental knowledge of the mixing and mastering process

What's Expected of You

The engineer's number one job is to "capture the magic" of the moment. That means all the technical aspects of the studio are set up and ready to go at a moment's notice.

This way, the artist and the producer can be completely focused on getting the best performances instead of worrying about the technical aspects of the recording process. The last thing a client ever wants to hear from you is "I wasn't ready" when they deliver a killer performance.

Record everything, even the warm-up runs or the rehearsals. You never know when something amazing will happen. As my good friend and Grammy-winning engineer Francis Buckley says, "ABR"—always be recording.

Another important job of the audio engineer is to take all of the raw recordings and piece them together in what's known as a "comp." A comp is when you take all of the different takes of a performance and cut and paste together the best bits, essentially creating one final "perfect" performance out of many "imperfect" performances.

You will also be responsible for cleaning up and getting rid of any extraneous noises, clicks, pops, buzzes, or hums. This way, when you deliver the final audio files, they are in pristine condition.

Acquaint yourself with the major pitch correction software on the market and familiarize yourself with how it works. It's becoming more and more routine to make sure everything is perfectly "in tune" on a project. People's ears are so used to hearing music so perfectly in tune these days, that when it's not in tune, they notice.

> The engineer's number one job is to "capture the magic" of the moment.
> That means all the technical aspects of the studio are set up
> and ready to go at a moment's notice.

Mixing

These days, the engineer that recorded the project may also be responsible for mixing it as well.

Mixing is the second to last step in the recording process. It requires you to take all the recorded material and bring it into *balance*, meaning all of the audio tracks work well with each other. Nothing is too loud; nothing is too quiet. It also requires you to create a sense of dimension and depth within the project.

There are hundreds of books and thousands of videos on the internet that offer advice on mixing. Everyone has a different opinion on the "correct" way of putting together a mix.

My advice is this: If you want to get better at mixing, learn the fundamentals of how sound works. Next, really listen attentively to songs you like and take them apart with your ears. Utilize a *reference mix* and try to mimic its overall character to achieve your balance.

This method will be slow at first, but the more you do it, the faster you'll be able to put together a mix that's balanced, punchy, and clear.

One more thing when mixing for a client. Make sure to get clarity on the direction they feel they want to go. Something that will absolutely help get you on the same page as your client will be to ask them for songs that they like the sound of and maybe would like to emulate. Again, referred to as a *reference mix*.

While you may not nail the mix on your first pass, the reference mix will help lead you in the right direction.

Revisions

One thing on which to count when you're mixing a project is *revisions* or sometimes referred to as *recalls*.

A first pass mix is rarely perfect. There will always be some form of adjustments for which the client will ask. This is completely normal.

After you submit your first version of a mix, give your client some time to sit with it. They'll likely listen to it on various sound systems and get back to you with any notes or adjustments they feel are necessary.

Hopefully, the adjustments will be small and easy to address. It's very rare that a client will want you to start over from scratch, but it does happen from time to time (usually, when the client has no earthly idea what they want). To avoid these situations, make sure the communication between you and your client is open and honest.

Even though revisions are an expected part of the mixing process, try to limit the amount for which your client is allowed to ask. When I'm mixing for a client, I allow for two revisions after the first mix is delivered. You can easily add a clause in your work-for-hire contract (see Chapter 4) that will limit the number of revisions allowed for the project.

If the client asks for more revisions than what we have agreed, I'll revert to an hourly rate for any additional updates. Again, this can be added to your work-for-hire so there are no surprises.

If you don't put a limit on the revisions, a client may continue to ask you to tweak the mixes for months on end until they feel the project is "finished." The problem with this is most artists will always hear something that needs to be "fixed," even if years have passed since the initial mix was started.

Mastering

Mastering is the final step in the recording process. While mixing is all about *balance*, mastering is all about *polish*.

A mastering engineer's job is very different from a mixing engineer. Mastering requires an entirely separate skillset from mixing.

The mastering engineer's job is to take all the final mixes from a project and elevate them to a *broadcast-ready* standard. This means getting the overall volume correct so a track can be competitive in the market, smoothing out any rough edges from the mixes, and helping to create a cohesive sound across an entire album's worth of material.

Adjustments are extremely subtle compared to a mix and require a level of hearing beyond the regular engineer.

A good mastering engineer can finish an entire album in a day. And unlike a mixing engineer, there are rarely any revisions. It's usually one and done.

Where to Find Engineering Gigs

Assuming you possess all the necessary equipment to record professional-sounding material, finding work as an engineer isn't as difficult as it may appear at first.

I'll assume that you may not possess enough equipment at the moment to record a full band. (If you do, just adapt this strategy to bands as well as solo artists.)

If you recall in Chapter 3, I used the idea of being an engineer/producer as an example of how to target some potential clients using *What? Who?* and *Where?*

Here's a refresher:

What: You're an engineer capable of recording, editing, and mixing and your goal is to find some potential new clients.

Who: Who needs an engineer that can record, edit, and mix? Singers, songwriters, hip-hop artists with no access to their own equipment.

Where: Where can you find some singers and songwriters? How about live shows? Open mic nights? Songwriting competitions?

Because an engineer doesn't have the luxury of showing off their skills in front of potential clients like a live playing musician does, it's going to take a bit more effort to get people to notice you.

Just follow the steps laid out in Chapter 3 to start networking in your local music scene. Remember, it may take some time for your efforts to start bearing fruit, but it's a necessary step.

You'll also need a website where you can showcase your skills to potential clients (see Chapter 4).

Another avenue is to join a website devoted to freelance-based workers like www.soundbetter.com or www.fiverr.com. Then create a profile and upload your demo reel. There is no guarantee that you will get any work from these sites, but you never know who may fortuitously find your profile.

The final way to go about finding engineering work would be to actually go to a local recording studio or postproduction facility and inquire about any potential internship opportunities.

While I have my own feelings about unpaid internships, it could be a way to get your foot in the door with a professional facility. Most will require you to submit some form of résumé (see Chapter 4) and conduct an interview. So be prepared.

Other Types of Engineering Gigs

You may equate being an audio engineer with music. However, if you are technically proficient at editing audio there are some other types of engineering gigs that you could also do. Here are some ideas:

- Postproduction audio/sound design for film and TV
- Podcast recording/editing
- Assisting YouTube creators with their sound and music
- Radio/broadcast
- Video games
- Audio books
- Overhead music for venues

As an engineer, try to keep an open mind about the gigs that are outside of recorded music. Some of these gigs actually pay better than most music engineering gigs.

Pay for Engineering Gigs

How and when you're paid for an engineering gig will be determined by the size and scope of the project for which you're hired.

Unless there is a "hard" deadline for delivering the project, it's not advisable to charge a "flat rate" for your services.

Charging by the hour or by the day allows for the extra time that is always necessary, whether recording or mixing.

Use the Hourly Rate formula in Chapter 3 to figure out your base line rate, double it, and negotiate from there.

If you can, try to get paid at the end of each workday, as it softens the financial blow to your client. If this isn't an option, remember not to release any work that you have done until you've been compensated for it.

Every now and then, you'll get an uppity client that insists that you send them something before they pay you. The problem here is even if you send them a low-quality MP3, there's a very good chance that it'll end up on SoundCloud and you'll be in the position of having to chase your client down for the money they owe you. You never want to be in the position of having to chase someone down—you want them to chase you.

So what do you do? Follow one of these three steps:

- Send them a snippet of the work you've done, perhaps, the first verse and half of the first chorus. Make hard edits on either end so it starts and stops abruptly. This will give them the opportunity to hear a sample of the work you've done, while not giving them anything usable.

- Send the complete track with an audio watermark. Record yourself saying something like "property of so and so" and drop it in throughout the track, preferably at key points in the song. This again, allows your client to hear your work, while still giving them something that is unusable.

- Turn the click track back on. This is by far my favorite option and the easiest. Send them the entire track, but turn the click track back on. This has worked without fail for some time for me. The client will call me and say, "Hey, I think you left the click track on." To which you reply, "Oh sorry, I'm sitting in front of my computer right now. If you can take care of the invoice I sent you, I'll send it right over." This makes your client come to you with something that they want. And you're willing and able to make it happen. They just need to take care of their business first. Try it next time you find yourself in this situation.

STUDIO CHECKLIST—ENGINEER

Session Information

Band/Artist: _____ Date(s): _____

Studio: _____ Address: _____

Producer: _____ Contact Info: _____

Of Songs: _____ Live Instruments? _____Yes/No_____

Start/End Time: _____ Hourly/Day Rate: _____

Engineer Checklist

☐ Portable Hard Drive ☐ Backup Hard Drive ☐ iLok w/licenses

☐ Microphones ☐ Mic Cables ☐ Pitch Correction Soft

☐ Mixing? ☐ Mix References ☐ Headphones

☐ Work-for-Hire Contract

Song Information

Song Title: _____ DAW: _____

Bit Depth/Sample Rate: _____ Tempo: _____

Additional Information or Requests

_____

_____

_____

_____

_____

Figure 6.3. Studio Checklist—Engineer
Author

Working as a Producer

The term *producer* gets thrown out a lot these days, without a basic understanding of what it actually means to be a music producer.

Unless the producer is also the artist, the main job of the producer is to understand the overall "vision" of the client or the artist that has hired you and make it happen. This entails navigating a project through its creative process from start to finish.

It could involve bringing in the right musical team, finding songs or songwriters that fit the vision of the project, or bringing in the right mixing and mastering engineers to help deliver the final product.

Or it could just be one person—you doing all of the above. The number of resources a producer can have at their disposal is directly proportional to the size and scope of the budget a client is willing to put forth.

Two Types of Producers

There are two overarching types of music producers in the world: the "hands-on" producer, and the "hands-off" producer.

Both types of producers should have an extensive knowledge of how a project is put together correctly and know the role each moving part plays within a production. The hands-on producer is normally down in the trenches making beats, finding sounds, directing performances, tracking vocals, and editing files.

The hands-off producer takes a more imaginative approach to making a record. While they may also have a vast knowledge of the technical process, they opt to instead act as almost a spiritual advisor, allowing their team to handle any technical aspects.

You may be wondering what good is the hands-off producer if they're not turning knobs and riding faders?

The answer is simple—they're there to get their artists to perform.

Performance Is Everything

While having a technical expertise of how a recording session works is valuable, that alone doesn't make a great producer.

What makes a great producer is getting down to the essence of a song or a project. It's understanding the artist's perspective and empathizing, then using that information to help guide their performance.

With today's technology, it's easy to fabricate a "perfect" performance—one that's in time and in tune. But what good is a perfect performance if it doesn't make the hair on your arms stand at attention or give you such an emotional gut punch that it takes you a minute to recover?

Everyone has a song or two in their life that they don't just hear; they *feel* it. This is the magic of recording, the elusive dragon that all producers chase, and some never catch . . . to capture that one amazing moment in time that makes everyone in the room go "Whoa!"

This magic requires the artist to give everything they've got to their performance. The only way this can be possible is if there is an immense amount of trust between the artist and the producer. It's the producer's job to cultivate this trust.

The producer needs to understand who the artist is, what they are trying to say, and why they want to say it. This requires the producer to get to know their artists and develop an almost intimate relationship (minus the physical).

I've had an artist call me at 3:00 a.m. to tell me they had a fight with their boyfriend and just need to talk to someone. I'll answer the phone and empathize with them. The next time we're in the studio and I need to get them to deliver an emotional performance, I may bring up our late-night conversation to see if I can get them to tap into the emotional center of how they felt that night. Once I feel that they're there, I press "record."

Expanding on the Core Skills

In addition to the Three Core Skills discussed in Chapter 3, to be an effective producer, you will need to add two more essential skills: the ability to articulate and the ability to make decisions.

The Ability to Articulate

As a producer, the ability to articulate means you are able to identify any issues or problems that may arise during the course of a project and convey clearly what is and is not working. You must also be able to explain in detail the solution to any problems that may occur.

Here's an example: The guitarist is rushing their part, causing the groove to feel too frantic.

Don't say something like "You're playing the part all wrong!"

This doesn't explain the core of the issue at hand and will probably cause the guitarist to feel stressed out, which could lead to more issues.

Do say, "It feels like you're playing a little on top of the beat."

This brings you to the next skill, which is one of the core skills.

The Ability to Communicate

In this situation you will need to communicate the problem with the guitarist in a way that won't shut them down. Artists and musicians are fragile creatures, so when you address a problem, you need to consider the personality of the person you're addressing. With some people, you can be forthright and honest, while others may need to be handled with kid gloves.

Understanding the personalities of the people with whom you work is extremely important. Saying the wrong thing the wrong way to an artist may derail an entire project.

Going back to the example with the guitarist who's rushing . . .

Try to say something like this: "Hey, you're sounding great, *and* on this next take lean back a little in your chair, take a breath, and loosen up the groove a bit."

Notice the use of the word "and" instead of "but." Somewhere, at some point in time, someone once said that anything that precedes the word "but" is bullshit. Using "but" would negate the genuine praise of "sounding great." By using "and," you're combining the praise with the instructions for getting what you need from them. It's a subtle thing. Try it out the next time you're put in a position like this. You may be surprised how effective it is.

As you work with more clients over time, this will become second nature. You'll learn when it's the right time to push someone and when to back off.

The Ability to Make Decisions

The last additional skill to develop as a producer is the ability to "make decisions."

It's easy to overlook this skill if the majority of your experience has been producing your own projects. At some point as a producer, you will have to decide to move on to get your projects finished.

The ability of effective decision-making was much easier in the days of analog recording. There was no "undo" button. If you got a good performance, you had to really ask yourself if it was worth risking the good performance to possibly get a better one. Once you recorded over a previous take on tape, it was gone forever.

In a strange way, having these limitations could actually help the decision-making process. With today's contemporary recording software, you now have an unlimited number of takes and multiple options at your disposal to enhance each performance; it's easy to become overwhelmed with too many choices.

In the early part of my career, I would become so hindered by the number of options I would have on any given project, that many of them ended up abandoned and unfinished.

Deciding is difficult because you can become so concerned with making the "right" decision, that you fail to make any at all.

Voltaire had a saying that can help break you from this mindset.

"Better is the enemy of good."

If something sounds "good" and "feels good," then it probably is good. Where we get into trouble is when we think we can outdo ourselves on the next take. Sometimes, we can; most times, we can't.

To avoid falling into this rabbit hole, the producer needs to know when enough is enough and make the decision that they have what they need, then move on to the next thing.

By nature, musicians are indecisive beings. And when you put a group of them in a room together, a project can find itself in the weeds quickly. A good producer should never lose sight of the overall vision of the project and will need to always maintain a sense of perspective with what's going on in the studio.

Developing your decision-making skills takes both time and experience. Making poor choices and learning from them is just as important as making the good ones. You can practice this by finding an abandoned project of yours and resolve to finish it, no matter what. Give yourself a deadline, and force yourself to make decisions until the project is finished. With each project you finish, your confidence in your ability to make clear and correct decisions will start to grow.

Pay for Producers

A producer can be paid in a number of ways, depending on the type of project it is and if there is a predetermined budget.

If you're working as an independent producer, developing undiscovered talent or local singers/songwriters, chances are the budget will be whatever they can pay you. In these situations, it's best to work with either an hourly or a daily rate. You'll get the most bang for your buck with the time you spend this way.

If the project has a dedicated budget, there are a few approaches to take.

"All-In" Budgets

An *all-in budget* is when a client has a set amount of money for the entire project. That means the cost of recording, marketing, mixing, mastering, musicians, and your personal fee are all tied into the budget.

If you're a savvy producer and are able to keep the recording costs down, you will earn a larger fee.

If the project goes off the rails and requires more time and effort than originally anticipated, it can severely impact the money with which you will walk away.

This is why it's so important for a producer to keep things on track and moving forward. You should try to account for unforeseen circumstances, but more often than not, something comes up that no one anticipated that makes an impact on the overall budget.

If your project is an all-in project, it's up to you to make sure everything comes in on time and on budget.

Fee-Based Budgets

A *fee-based budget* is fairly straightforward. You are guaranteed a specific amount of money no matter how bloated a project may become. Fee-based budgets will sometimes pay you a portion of your fee up front and the rest at the end of the project.

For longer projects, there may be a *milestone* system in place.

A *milestone* system is when you're paid a portion of your fee based on reaching certain milestones within the project. For instance, you may get 20% of your fee when you start, another 20% when you deliver the first batch of recordings, and then another 20% when you reach the mixdown phase.

This can be a good system to work with if a project looks as though it may take many months to complete. This way, you're continuously earning throughout the course of the project. If you're paid everything up front, you may have the urge to spend it right away and end up in a financial lurch six months later.

Back End

As the producer on certain projects, you may be entitled to what's referred to as *back end*.

Back end is royalties or residuals made on how well the project performs in the marketplace. If you've also written or cowritten any songs for the project, you'll be entitled to mechanical and performance royalties as well (see Chapter 5).

Regardless of whether you wrote any songs or not, the producer may sometimes earn what's known as *points* on a record or a project. A *point* is 1% of every dollar the project earns in sales. A normal record producer could expect as many as three points for a project. If you're Quincy Jones, you're getting five points or more.

Back in the day when consumers actually bought physical records, this could net the producer a lot of extra income. However, with the advent of online streaming services and digital downloads, the money from points isn't as good as it used to be. Nevertheless, points do still exist, so if offered, you may as well take them.

STUDIO CHECKLIST—PRODUCER

Session Information

Artist/Client:_____Contact Info: _____

Song/Project Title: _____ Delivery Date:_____

Project Budget: _____ Producer Fee/Rate: _____

Studio:_____ Studio Rate:_____

Live Musicians?_____Yes/No_____ Musician Rate: _____

Engineer/Mix?_____Yes/No_____ Engineer Rate: _____

Mastering Engineer? ____Yes/No____ Mastering Rate: _____

Producer Checklist

☐ Song/Project Structure   ☐ Tempo   ☐ Song/Project Key

☐ Lyrics/Lyric Sheet?   ☐ Arrangement   ☐ Instrumentation

☐ Producer Points?   ☐ Split Sheets   ☐ Track References?

☐ A Complete and Thorough Understanding of the Artist/Client's Vison for the Project?

Additional Information or Requests

_____

_____

_____

_____

_____

_____

Figure 6.4.   Studio Checklist—Producer
Author

Working as a Session Musician

Session musicians have been the backbone of the music industry for as long as it has been in existence. A session musician is at the top of their game in terms of technical proficiency, tone, and feel. They are also able to create within a track both memorable and moving performances.

If you listen to any records from Motown, Stax, Columbia, or Atlantic records from the early fifties through the seventies, chances are they will contain the same sets of musicians playing on records for multiple artists.

The same goes for film, TV, and music for games. Almost everything you hear in regard to these types of music is likely performed by the same small group of individuals.

A session musician's life is a life in the shadows. The only people that ever really get to know who they are, are most likely other musicians or producers that appreciate what they do. That's the gig though. You make everyone else sound better. (Check out the documentaries *The Wrecking Crew*, *Standing in the Shadows of Motown*, *20 Feet from Stardom*, and *Muscle Shoals* for some great stories about session singers and musicians.)

Skills Required

- The Three Core Skills (technical proficiency, a great ear, and the ability to communicate effectively), pushed to the limit of your ability

- A vast knowledge of different styles and techniques

- The ability to play it right and play it quickly (time is money)

- An uncanny sense of rhythm and timing (also the ability to play to a click track, while injecting feel and groove)

- The ability to read music (this is more for film and television sessions, explained below)

- A firm understanding of the technology used to create different sounds (FX pedals and the like)

- Knowledge of how to fix pitch and intonation issues related to your instrument quickly

What's Expected of You

As a session musician, your job is to enhance a project with your musicianship. At the most basic level, you must have an extraordinary sense of rhythm as well as the ability to understand what the project needs as far as tone and feel.

Normally, it's a producer's job to tell you what they're looking for. And depending on the producer's ability to articulate and communicate, this can sometimes pose a challenge. Often, a session musician will have to decipher the "code" of what's being asked of them.

I learned this lesson early on in one of my first big sessions. The producer kept yelling at me to "Make it hot!!!" What does that even mean? In a panic, I just started pushing buttons and turning on and off different pedals trying to make my sound "hot."

Eventually, I turned on a tap tempo delay that sounded like The Edge from U2, and the producer jumped out of his chair and said, "That's it; that's that fire shit!!!"

Obviously, it would have been easier for me if he just would have said, "Give me something like The Edge from U2."

From that moment on, whenever I had a session with him, I knew what "hot" meant. I even put a piece of masking tape on my delay pedal renaming it the "hot button."

A lot of the major producers these days have developed from using only their computers to make their music. There's nothing wrong with that, but a lot of them will lack the musical vocabulary with which most trained musicians are familiar. That makes it your job as a session musician to understand what they're after. At first, it can be frustrating dealing with these situations, but remember that not everyone may have the depth of musical knowledge you possess.

What helps is to ask the producer for a reference. I'll have them play some songs for me in which they like the guitar parts, and then I'll use them to emulate those parts and sounds to the best of my ability. Which brings me to my next point . . .

As a session musician, you are also going to need to be a bit tech savvy. If you play only an acoustic instrument, that's fine, but investing in some tech that can change and alter the sounds you create can open up some more work opportunities for you.

Tina Gao is a famous session cellist, who not only plays beautiful acoustic cello parts but will also run her instrument through a multitude of guitar effects' pedals to create some amazing and unique soundscapes. She plays on records, movie scores, and a lot of music for video games.

It's essential for you to understand what your equipment can and can't do. Sessions move fairly fast, so your ability to find and dial in the right sounds quickly can be the difference between your getting called to come in again or being replaced.

This is something you can practice at home on your own with no pressure. Open the current Top Ten playlist and see if you can emulate the sounds you hear. Time yourself to see how long it takes you to dial in a sound that's close. Do it again for the next song. Continue doing this every day until you're able to almost perceive the sound in your head before you even touch a pedal or knob.

The final and most important thing required for a session musician is their ability to interpret a performance, meaning the ability to inject feel and emotion into your parts.

Sometimes, you may be looking at a part that is written out in musical notation; your job is to take those notes and play them as though you've been playing them your entire life. Frequently, there will be no sheet music provided, so you will need to listen to the track, develop a part that works, and perform it as if it's always been there.

Things like phrasing, dynamics, and the attacks and releases of notes are all integral to creating a dynamic and memorable performance. Anyone can play a series of notes strung together, but a session musician's job is to make those notes speak.

Do You Need to Be Able to Read Music?

Yes! And no. If you want to play sessions for film and TV, your parts will almost certainly be written out by the composer, and you are expected to play them correctly.

Because most film and TV sessions are run by the American Federation of Musicians (AFM), the players are expected to nail their parts on either the first or, at most, second take. If you're unable to do this, you will be replaced. Production companies don't have the time (or money) to waste while you figure out your part.

When dealing with records and smaller projects, you may not even get a chord chart. Out of all the sessions I've done in my career for records, I've received perhaps two charts where the notation was actually written down for me. For the rest, I've had to rely solely on my ear to figure out the key and the chord changes.

Knowing how to read music is an extremely useful tool to possess. However, more and more these days, it's not as crucial as it was in the past for sessions. Don't take this as you shouldn't learn to read music—you absolutely should!

Developing a great ear and good musical instincts should be your first priority, as these two skills will carry you through most any session situation.

Tuning and Intonation

Make sure your instrument's tuning and "intonation" is spot on. And know how to adjust both quickly should they start to slip. A clip-on strobe tuner is a necessity for an active session musician.

Intonation, for those that don't know, is how well the instrument plays in tune across its entire musical range. Wooden instruments are susceptible to intonation problems more than most others. Things like heat, cold, and moisture can cause your instrument's intonation to slip.

Another tuning tip: Sometimes, the session will use a sample that has been pitched up or down and doesn't necessarily reside in one key or another. This is common on hip-hop sessions. It's important to recalibrate your tuner or the global tuning settings on your instrument to accommodate for these samples; otherwise, everything will sound slightly out of tune and not in a good way.

Finding Work as a Session Musician

Finding work as a session musician is not as straightforward as most other types of gigs. The most important thing you'll need to do is get yourself in front of some music producers and composers.

Very rarely will you be hired sight unseen for a session if you haven't developed a solid reputation yet. So the trick is to get acquainted with as many producers in your area as possible. Trouble is, many of them don't perform live, so it can be tough to meet them.

I was lucky in landing my first real sessions. I just happened to be playing at a club where a big music producer was just hanging out having dinner. Apparently, I piqued his interest, and the next day there I was doing a session for Interscope Records. Right time, right place. After that, my career as a session musician took off.

Playing live in your area is probably the fastest way to get noticed. You can also take advantage of things like social media to create content and showcase your playing abilities, then share them with producers and composers in your online communities.

There are also freelance services like www.soundbetter.com or www .fiverr.com, where you can promote yourself as a session musician. However, the quality of work may be low, but the more sessions you do, even the bad ones, will help you gain the necessary experience.

If your local colleges have a music production program or film composition classes, you may be able to find some work through them. Most colleges offer some form of a public forum where you could post your availability, but it's not a guarantee.

One thing that will help jump-start your session career is versatility. Having the ability to play as many styles as possible convincingly is very attractive to a music producer. Also, playing a unique instrument can open doors faster than just being a guitarist.

For instance, if you're a guitarist but can also play mandolin, banjo, and ukulele, these will immediately up your value in the eyes of someone thinking of hiring you.

Tommy Tedesco was one of the most recorded session guitarists ever. His is a legend among the session musician community. He was known to be able to play any stringed and fretted instrument amazingly well. Because of this, he was never out of work. Later in his life, when asked how he could be so good on so many instruments, he confessed that he would just tune them all like a guitar so he didn't have to learn any new fingerings or chord shapes. Absolute genius! The point is, he was able to adapt to any job that became available. While some session musicians get known for their thing, having the ability to adapt to different musical styles, as well as different instruments, will keep you in demand.

One last thing: If you have the ability to record high-quality tracks from your home studio, you can greatly expand on your list of potential clients. I've done sessions for clients in Japan, Korea, and Germany, all from the comfort of my home. Just make sure you get paid *before* you start sending out the files from the sessions.

There is no fast track to becoming a session musician unless you already know someone who needs one. Work on building your reputation through playing live shows with as many different musicians as possible. Eventually, some of them are going to want to do some recording, and hopefully they'll ask you to be a part of it.

> One thing that will help jump-start your session career is versatility. Having the ability to play as many styles as possible convincingly is very attractive to a music producer.

Pay for Session Musicians

The money you earn as a session musician will vary depending on the project. Sessions under the purview of the AFM tend to pay the best. Union rates are standardized, and you can make a very good living playing on film, TV, and video game sessions.

The going rate for a union session at the time of this writing (2022) is $450 for a three-hour session. That doesn't include things like doubles (playing a different instrument or overdubbing extra parts) and overtime.

These are high-pressure sessions that will usually require you to be a great reader. They are also extremely exclusive to get into. Even if you are a member of the union, these sessions are typically reserved for the musicians with the most experience and time invested as a member.

There is a joke that says in order to get into these sessions, someone has to die. The sad part is, it's somewhat true. You can truly earn a good living doing these types of sessions, and the musicians doing them are very reluctant to give them up. I've been on some sessions where the members of the orchestra were pushing upward of eighty years old. Amazing! I can understand their point of view—good, steady work as a musician is hard to come by. So when you find it, you hold onto it for dear life.

The majority of session work these days is not regulated by the union, and therefore it's every person for themselves.

Because there is no standard rate for freelance sessions, it has caused a drop in what you can expect to be paid. Working on an hourly rate may seem smart, but if you're really good at what you do and it only takes you an hour to record everything, you could end up making less than someone who is not as proficient as you are.

The way I handle my freelance sessions is I charge hourly but with a minimum of at least four hours. So even if I finish everything in an hour, I'll still be paid for four. If the session goes beyond the four hours, then I'll revert back to charging for every extra hour I'm there.

Come up with a rate that works for you based on a minimum number of hours and adjust when necessary.

Hopefully, this gives you an idea of how to charge for your sessions, but getting the money into your account is a different matter. This is where the union is handy. They make sure everyone gets paid for the sessions; you never really have to worry with them on your side. Freelance gigs, on the other hand, can be a little more precarious.

In my early days of doing session work, I had to invoice the record label for my rates. That meant I would have to wait for the label to approve my invoice, cut a check, and then mail it out. It was not a quick process. One session took nine months to pay me! Nine months!

Most sessions today are operating with a very small budget if any. This means that you will likely be paid by the producer or the artist directly. This can be a good thing because you will be paid much quicker than if you had to invoice a record label. However, you should always be paid before you leave the session; otherwise, you'll be chasing people for your money, which as I've said, is a position you never want to be in.

If you're going to someone else's studio, you're not in control of the recordings; therefore, you won't have the leverage of holding the work hostage. You're going to have to trust that you will be taken care of. Even if you have a contract with the producer, that doesn't always guarantee that they will pay you in a timely manner. It's best to make it known before you arrive that you would like to be paid when the session is over. If they have a problem with that, you may want to think twice before going.

I always give a producer the benefit of the doubt—once. And more often than not, I'm taken care of in a timely fashion. However, if a producer tries to jerk me around or ducks my phone calls, I won't deal with them ever again. And I'll make sure all my session musician buddies know not to deal with them either. Reputation goes both ways.

The final thing about pay for sessions: Working as a session musician at any level is considered "work-for-hire" (see Chapter 4). You do your job, get paid, go home. You have no creative stake in the content you add to the project.

This also means there is no *back end* with sessions, other than a possible mechanical royalty. Keep this in mind while you're on the session. I've had situations where I show up and the producer has left the bridge of the song blank and asks me to create something cool to fill it. Be wary of these situations. This is where being a session musician begins crossing over into being a writer on the song. If you go ahead and create something, you're still under a work-for-hire contract. And if that song becomes a hit, you won't get anything other than your pay for the session.

Whenever something like this comes up, and it does more often than you may think, be prepared. Sure, part of being a session musician is creating parts that weren't originally there, but if you're asked to create a whole section of a song from nothing, that's writing.

If this occurs, I will stop what I'm doing and have a conversation with the producer or the artist and explain that if they want me to "make up a bridge," we need to amend my work-for-hire agreement and discuss any *splits* on the composition of the song. I will still make my session rate but will require that I also be added as a writer on the song.

If they don't agree to this, tell the producer they need to come up with the part, and you'll be happy to play on top of it. I made this mistake often early in my career. It cost me a lot of money in royalties. I'm embarrassed to admit how much.

STUDIO CHECKLIST—SESSION MUSICIAN

Session Information

Band/Artist:_____ Date(s):_____

Studio:_____ Address: _____

Producer:_____ Contact Info: _____

Of Songs: _____ Multiple Instruments?_____Yes/No_____

Start/End Time:_____ Hourly/Day Rate:_____

Session Musician Checklist

☐ Instrument(s) ☐ Cables   ☐ Power Supplies

☐ Tuner   ☐ Extra Accessories ☐ Blank Paper (staff)

                 ☐ Work-for-Hire Contract

Song Information

Song Title:_____ Song Key: _____

Song Form: _____

Song Chord Changes:_____

_____

_____

Additional Song Information

_____

_____

_____

_____

_____

Figure 6.5.   Studio Checklist—Session Musician
Author

TYPES OF COMPOSING GIGS AND GIG PROTOCOLS AND TEACHING

Public Domain

Working as a Media Composer

A media composer creates music for the sole purpose of its being combined with some other form of media—film, TV, advertising, or games. Frequently, a media composer's music is used to help tell the story that's appearing on screen or to help the audience feel the "correct" emotion with the visuals they are seeing. Putting the "wrong" type of music against a particular scene of a film can result in a "disconnect" between the viewer and the intention of the film's or game's director. It is vitally important that a media composer, much like a music producer, fully understand and interpret the *vision* of the director of a project.

Skills Required

- The Three Core Skills (again with an emphasis on communication)

    ○ Technical proficiency

    ○ A great ear

    ○ The ability to communicate with others

- An understanding of technical specifications for composing, such as SMPTE time code, frame rates, and sample rates

- The ability to create the correct mood or emotion for a given scene

- A fundamental understanding of creating memorable themes and motifs, with the ability to develop them across a project's timeline

- The ability to create realistic *mock-ups* of your music for demo purposes

Music for Film and Television

The most high-profile media composer gig is the film composer. Think Hans Zimmer or Danny Elfman—big names associated with blockbuster movies. A film composer works closely with a director or the producers of a film or TV show to get to the essence of what the overall mood of a project should be.

On a full-length feature film, a composer may be required to create as much as ninety minutes of music to tie a picture together. A television show or series may require between twenty and fifty minutes of music per episode. If a show has ten episodes, that is a lot of music that needs to be created.

If that doesn't sound stressful enough, music is typically one of the last things added to a project, leaving you very little time to create what may be needed.

Cues

The good news about having to create such an immense amount of music in a short period of time is that you aren't expected to create everything at once.

A film score gets broken down into what are known as *cues*. Cues are essentially short pieces of music that once pieced together, will give you the entire scope of the score.

This makes the job of scoring much more manageable, as you will focus your time in smaller three- to five-minute chunks, as opposed to trying to manage sixty minutes of music all at once. Once a cue is written, it is then placed at the correct *time code* within the film, creating *sync* (synchronization) between the picture and the music.

Where a particular cue is placed within a film is decided on by the director in what's known as the *spotting session.*

A spotting session is where you (the composer) and either the director, showrunner, or producers of the project watch a *cut* of the film and decide where there should and shouldn't be music.

Most *rough cuts* of a film will have a group of numbers burned into the picture while watching. This is referred to as *BITC*, or *burnt-in timecode*. The numbers are laid out like this: 00.00.00.00. Each decimal point refers to a specific timing broken down by *hours.minutes.seconds. frames*. Using this time code allows for the ability to *sync* up the music to the picture perfectly.

The director may say something like *"At 01.23.55.08, I want the music to swell in, but then at 01.25.32.15, I want the music to be out."*

This gives you an accurate idea of exactly where your music will start and where it needs to finish.

You will continue through the entire film discussing where music starts and stops, what type of music, the instrumentation, the mood and feel, and so on.

As you go through your spotting session, it's important to take very detailed notes. I recommend also recording the spotting session as a voice memo on your phone, just so you don't miss anything the director may ask for. Which brings us to our next subject . . .

Communicating with a Director

What does purple sound like?

The biggest obstacle you will face when working with either film directors or TV producers is the musical language barrier. While they may speak in terms of *feel* and *emotion*, composers tend to speak in more musical terms like *major* or *minor*.

Some directors will have a basic musical vocabulary that they will use to convey their point, but most don't. It's very important to understand that you should not try to impose your musical vocabulary on them. In my experience, it can cause frustration between you and the director.

You, as the composer, need to try to understand what the director means when they say something like, *"This scene feels cold."* Cold to a musician can mean many things but not necessarily what the director has in mind.

To overcome the language barrier, listen carefully to what they are saying. Try to internalize the emotions they are trying to convey. Offer examples of what "cold" may mean to you using other movies or music that they may know as a reference point. Doing this allows the two of you to go through a process of elimination to truly get to the heart of what the director envisions for the scene.

It may take a few meetings to get to the core understanding. Try not to get frustrated; directors are typically very passionate about their projects. Remember that it's your job to help them realize their complete vision and not the other way around.

The "Mock-Up"

Once you've gotten your direction and received a *locked cut* (a final edited version) of the film, you will need to import it into your DAW of choice to begin the work. Make sure you ask for both the *frame rate* (number of frames per second, 30fps is standard for the United States) and the *sample rate* (number of audio samples recorded per second; for film and television, the standard is 48 kHz, or 48,000 samples per second) of the video file they give you. This is to make sure that the music will *sync* perfectly with the video.

When it's time to start writing, unless the project has a major budget that allows for the hiring of an orchestra, you will need to create what's known as a *mock-up* of what the final music will sound like.

Creating a mock-up means that you will be responsible for creating all of the instruments and parts that they play within your computer, most likely using samples. The good news is, there are lots of great sample libraries on the market today that can help bring a sense of realism and even grandeur to your mock-up.

Creating a realistic-sounding mock-up will help give the director a sense of what the final music will sound like, therefore, allowing them to make suggestions on what is working and what isn't, without wasting money on an orchestra.

Once the director is happy with the direction, budget allowing, you will move on to rerecording all of the parts with live musicians. This, however, is typically reserved for the big-budget blockbuster movies and shows.

Most TV shows and a lot of films rely almost entirely on a sample-based orchestra, as their budgets don't allow for the hiring of a sixty-piece orchestra. So you will need to make sure your mock-up sounds as close to the real thing as possible. Making a sample-based orchestra sound convincing takes a lot of time and practice, utilizing things like *expression, modulation, key switches,* and *dynamic control* of the sampled instruments.

One way to practice your programming skills is to take a famous piece of classical music, locate the full score, and program in all of the parts—all the while listening to what sounds "real" and what doesn't. From there, start adjusting the different parameters of the samples to add a sense of realism and feel.

Your ability to create a realistic sounding mock-up can mean the difference in getting the gig or not. Just like learning an instrument, you will need to devote time, discipline, and practice to really get the hang of it.

Finding Film Composing Gigs

Finding your first film composing gigs can be easier than you may think. Most colleges have some sort of film study program where the students are required to shoot their own short films.

Young directors relish the opportunity to work with a composer on their projects. Having a bespoke score for their short film can make their project feel more special as opposed to just superimposing the *Gladiator* soundtrack over it.

The early films you do will likely be for "experience" as opposed to making money. However, some schools have the students go out and raise money as they would on a real film and create a budget. This may include a small budget for the music.

When I first moved to LA, I got involved with some of the students at the American Film Institute. I haphazardly scored the music for a student's short film, and I was paid around $500 for it. What I wasn't aware of at the time was that they held a screening of the film at the school for the other students. The next thing I knew, I was getting a lot of calls from other directing students asking me to score their films too. Each film had a relatively small budget, and I ended up making anywhere between $500 and $1,500 per short film.

Even if there were no money involved with these projects, I still would have done them. These were low-pressure situations where I could make a mistake and it wouldn't ruin my reputation. All the while, I was building my skills as a composer and communicator.

Working with film students will be the fastest way for you to gain the experience necessary to move on to larger projects. It will also help you build confidence in your work and prepare you for the challenges of bringing a director's vision to life.

Another avenue for an aspiring composer to take would be working as an assistant for an already established composer. The trouble is, when these positions do become available, they normally aren't advertised publicly. Most assistant gigs come with a recommendation, so it really boils down to who you know. Joining online communities of movie producers, directors, and editors can lead to rumblings that a certain composer is looking for a new assistant. Joining an organization like SCL (Society of Composers and Lyricists; www.thescl.com) can put you in the orbit of some working composers as well.

Signing up for an online class for composing could also introduce you to other working composers that may come in as guest speakers. This will give you a chance to inquire if they need someone.

You may also find an opportunity by either contacting the composer directly (which I don't fully advise) or finding who their manager is and inquiring with them.

The truth of the matter is, if you want to work as an assistant for a working composer, you have to go where the working composers are. That means LA or New York. There are a few big-name composers who live outside these areas; however, if you want to work as a composer for film and TV, you may need to think about making the move to where the work is.

Pay for a Film/TV Composer

Budgets for film and television gigs operate very much like a budget for a record. Most composers receive what's known as a *package deal*. The package deal is the same as an *all-in* budget for a record, meaning recording costs, hiring musicians, and your pay are all rolled into one.

But how do you know what you should be charging? If you're doing student films, you really should take whatever they can offer, as there probably isn't much wiggle room within their budgets for the music. Sometimes, they won't be able to offer you anything, and then it becomes your decision as to whether or not to continue. If you're just starting out, I would advise you to take the gig for the "experience"; it will pay off later.

If there is a budget and you're being asked to create around sixty minutes of original music, how do you figure out how much sixty minutes of your music is worth?

You can use the Hourly Rate Calculator (see Chapter 3) with a few small adjustments to figure this out. Most composers charge per minute of music. So instead of figuring out how much one hour of your time is worth, you're figuring out how much one minute of your music is worth.

To figure this out, you'll first need to realistically assess how many minutes of finished music you can complete in one day.

Here's a frame of reference: Some of the best composers in the business get around only five to six minutes of completed music per day. So it's safe to say that a composer of moderate skill should be able to get about half of that—say, two to three minutes.

- Okay, you can feasibly do two minutes of music a day. To finish the full sixty minutes, it would take you around thirty days of work.

- Now, figure out your survival budget (again) for each month, for instance, $2,000/month.

  ○ Double it to $4,000/month. Now, divide by the number of working days, Monday–Friday (20 days).

  ○ $4,000/20 days = $200 per day. Take your day rate and divide by the number of minutes of music you can do per day: $200/two minutes = $100 per minute.

- At this rate, the cost for you to do sixty minutes of music should be around $6,000 minimum.

If the production is taking care of the recording costs, this is a great way to get a ballpark figure on what your fee should be. If anything, it will give you a place from which to negotiate.

If you have a package deal, my advice would be to add another 50% on top of your fee to cover things like recording costs, mixing, or mastering.

- $6,000 × 50% = $3,000

- Total package budget: $6,000 (fee) + $3,000 (extra costs) = $9,000 for a package deal

Keep in mind that when you're starting out, you may not be able to demand much if any money. That doesn't mean that you shouldn't try to get something for your efforts.

The Demo Reel

One thing that is necessary for a composer to have is a great *demo reel*. A demo reel is a collection of your work condensed into a short, easily accessible format, such as a YouTube video or .mov file, that you can send to a director to showcase your talent.

If you're just starting out, finding original video content to score can be difficult. A good way to start putting a reel together is to take something that already exists, and rescore it. This could be a trailer or a scene from a movie that has already been released. You can pull the video file from sites like YouTube or Vimeo, remove the original audio, and replace it with your own. Not only is this a great way to get your demo reel going, but it's great practice for scoring different types of scenes. Once you've scored the scene, remove the video, and add the audio to your reel. Using a well-known movie scene to promote your work isn't advisable, but you can use them as a catalyst for your ideas.

The best way to approach putting together your demo reel is to keep it short and to the point, no longer than three minutes. Have at least three one-minute pieces that showcase your versatility, but do try to keep the overall feel consistent, meaning try not to jump around through too many different genres. It's not a bad idea to create multiple demo reels for showcasing different styles.

You always want to lead with your strongest material. This is the first impression that a potential client will get from you, so you want to impress them right away. Make sure your reel feels cohesive in the way it moves from piece to piece. This may require you to adjust and edit your music so it fits together seamlessly.

Try your best to make your reel sound as "expensive" as possible. Most clients don't understand the difference between a "demo" and a "final product." They will just hear a demo that sounds unfinished and assume that this is the type of music that they will receive if they hire you. Don't give them that option. Once you get the gig, you can freely submit unfinished ideas because everyone involved on the project understands that you are working toward a finished product for them.

Once you have a finished demo reel, upload it to your website so it can be streamed easily on the internet. It's safe to say that almost everyone in the music business and beyond has no desire to download a large file containing your demo reel. Make the process easy for a potential client to find and view your work via the internet; they're much more likely to click on a link rather than download an email attachment.

Production Music Library Music

A lot of productions these days are forgoing hiring a composer and relying instead on finding music for their projects using what's known as a *production music library.*

A production music library is a database of hundreds to thousands of pieces of music that are written in advance with no specific project in mind. The music is categorized by concepts like mood, instrument, tempo, and so forth. Most music libraries are searchable via *tags* embedded in the *metadata* of the file.

For instance, if a director wants a piece of music for their project, they could type in terms such as "cheerful," "acoustic," and "guitar." The database then filters the search results to show only pieces that are tagged with those terms, therefore, narrowing down the search.

While films and games still tend to hire composers to create a bespoke score, productions like reality TV shows, commercials, corporate training videos, and internet and radio advertisements are more and more using a production music library to find what they need.

While library music has been around for a long time, in the past decade its use has skyrocketed. The shift to more "reality-style" shows and internet streaming services has contributed to its rise in popularity for a couple of reasons. The first is, using library music is typically cheaper than hiring a composer. Two, obtaining a license is relatively easy. And three, instead of writing the music to the picture, a production company will more often than not edit the picture to the music.

Using library music can also cut down on the time a project spends in postproduction, therefore saving the company a lot of money.

Getting Started in Production Music Library Music

Because of their growing popularity, there are now many large music libraries in existence that contain hundreds of thousands of pieces of music, all *tagged*, all searchable. Do a Google search of "Production Music Libraries," and you should get a list of the current heavy hitters.

A lot of major record labels like Universal Music Group and Warner Chappell Music have also thrown their massive hats into the library game, making it difficult for smaller independent libraries to get noticed.

The good news is that most of the major music libraries, minus the record labels, are reasonably open to new composers submitting their music. The bad news is, you need to have a fairly exhaustive list of material before they will even consider you. Music libraries look at composers like a numbers game. The more composers and material they have, the more likely they'll be able to license and make money off of them.

However, don't think that because it's relatively easier to submit to a library that they'll just accept any old piece of music. There are protocols and requirements for submissions, the most important being that your tracks have to sound professional and finished, meaning they could grab your piece of music, plop it into a show, and they're done. *There is no room or time for demos in library music.*

Make sure that before you submit or *pitch* your music to a library, it sounds *broadcast ready.*

Tips for Production Music Library Success

While each library may have some different protocols for how they handle their music, there are some universal standards that they all abide by.

Following these standards from the start can greatly enhance the possibility that your music will be picked up.

- Make sure the music is *broadcast ready*.

- Keep your tracks under three minutes long. One minute thirty seconds to two minutes is optimal.

- Follow an A, B, A structure. Start with an idea, change to something else, then readdress the initial idea with more musical *development*.

- Add edit points every thirty seconds. Create a *break* in the music every thirty seconds or so. This allows an editor to cut and possibly rearrange the music to fit the scene on which they are working.

- Create a thirty-second version for use in commercials (twenty-eight seconds in the United Kingdom).

- Make *stems* of each instrument group. Stems (short for "stereo masters") are files separated by an instrument or a group of instruments. For instance, a drum stem would consist of all the percussive elements. A keyboard stem would contain only the keyboard elements. And so on and so on for each instrument group.

  ○ When the stems are lined up in a new session and played back, you should hear the final piece of music as it was intended. Creating stems allows for greater flexibility with the music. For instance, if the director likes everything but the drums, if they have the stems, they can remove them and use the remaining stems to get what they want.

- Learn the naming protocols of the library. It may be something like "Sunrise(title)_95bpm(tempo)_Amin(key)_Sad (mood)_24/48(sample rate)." Each library will have its own naming protocols, with which you should familiarize yourself.

- Embed the *metadata* for the track. The metadata within the files is how the tracks become searchable within a database.

This is where you can *tag* the track with any relative search terms based on mood, tempo, key, feel, and so on. It's also obligatory to embed all of your personal information, such as your name, your publisher, your PRO information (ASCAP, BMI, etc.), and any *splits* with other writers. Most DAW's have the ability to add this information to your files while exporting. Familiarize yourself with this process. It's absolutely necessary if you want to be paid for mechanical uses and streaming.

The big thing to remember when you sit down and write music for a library is that it needs to evoke a mood or a feeling, the same as if you were writing music for a film, the biggest difference being that you won't have someone guiding you as to what they're looking for. This can be both frustrating and liberating at the same time. When composing library music, I sit down with a mood in mind. It may be with the intention of writing some upbeat, pop/rock tracks, or I may be feeling a little melancholy, so I write something moody.

The point is, as long as it evokes a feeling, it has the potential to be used in a production. So write whatever you feel in the moment.

There is no room or time for demos in library music.

The Music Supervisor

Most films and TV shows have what's known as a music supervisor. The music supervisor's job is to work closely with a director to find and place preexisting music that is appropriate for the project.

The music supervisor is the gatekeeper for getting your library music into a project. They will search through hundreds of potential tracks looking for that perfect one that will fit the scene on which they're working.

Because the music supervisor is responsible for the clearing and licensing of tracks, which can be a complicated process, they tend to have a number of go-to libraries that they always use. Rarely, do they seek out music that is outside of their usual channels.

Getting your music into a larger library with a proven track record will make it more likely that a music supervisor may stumble upon your music.

The downside is that you may get lost in a sea of other composers that have their music with the same library. The way you can combat being buried is to constantly submit new material to your library. It's a numbers game. The more tracks you have available, the greater the chances of their being found and used.

I would advise against directly contacting a music supervisor. They know they hold the keys to getting your music placed. They also know that every songwriter and composer in the industry is desperate to get their music licensed. Unless you personally know a music supervisor, I truly advise against reaching out directly.

However, if you want to get a bit creative, put yourself in a position to "bump into" some music supervisors. You could sign up for an organization like the Guild of Music Supervisors (www.guildofmusicsupervisors .com). It may cost you some money to join, but the upside is you can attend meetings and functions that the organization puts on and get some much-needed face time in front of the right people.

The Editor

There are some types of shows that don't even have a music supervisor—think most types of reality TV.

While the director or showrunner still has final say as to what the music should be, more and more it's become a show's music editor that digs around for the proper music.

The main job of the editor is to cut all the video footage together for a show. For many reality-type shows (think *History Channel*, *Discovery Channel*, etc.) the editor will find and pull music tracks from a library and cut them into the show. This cuts down the production time of a show, while having the added benefit of not having to pay a music supervisor.

The first placements I ever had in a show were because of the editor. He was a keyboard player in a band I was in but worked as an editor for the *Discovery Channel* for his day gig.

One day he randomly asked me if I had any "swampy guitar" tracks. I didn't. But I said I did. I went home and made a few and sent them in, and he cut them into the show he was working on. Just like that, I became a composer for film and television.

It's been over a decade now since that first placement, and I still send him tracks whenever he needs something.

Finding editors can be as difficult as finding music supervisors. Most of them will reside in either LA or New York.

Like music supervisors, editors also have a "guild" that they belong to—the Motion Picture Editors Guild (www.editorsguild.com), which is open to new members. They also hold seminars and networking events for their members that you could attend.

The Pay for Production Music Library Music

There are a few factors to consider when discussing the pay for getting your library music placed.

The first would be any up-front licensing fees for the use of your music, more commonly known as a *sync fee*. A sync fee can range anywhere from $50 to $50,000, depending on the popularity and demand for the track.

If you're working independently and personally licensing your own music, you are entitled to the entire sync fee. If your music is part of a larger library or you have a publishing deal with a third party, you may either split the fee or not see any of it at all. Make sure you read any agreements when dealing with larger libraries or music publishers. Don't ever be afraid to ask for clarification when dealing with licenses.

It's normal to split the fee with a larger library. Libraries make their money by promoting your music, so consider it the cost of doing business with them.

In addition to any up-front fees you may receive for the use of your music, as the composer you are also entitled to any performance royalties that your tracks may generate. This is why it's so important to make sure that you are signed up with a PRO (ASCAP, BMI, SESAC, etc.) as both a *writer* and a *publisher* and have all of your material registered with them in order to collect the full amount of royalties.

If you are working with a music library or a music publisher, it's more than likely that they will receive the publisher's share of your royalties, while you will still collect your writer's share. Each company is different in the way they handle royalty distribution, so make sure that you look closely at any contract you sign when you begin working with them.

Licenses

A license is granted by the owner of a piece of music's copyright for a film or television show to use their music. There are two main types of licenses, and depending on which one is requested, the size of the sync fee may vary.

The first and most common license is referred to as *nonexclusive*. A nonexclusive license means that a show or film wants to use your music but will allow you the ability to license the music to any other interested parties. Because you can freely license the same music to anyone else that's interested, the sync fee is typically lower.

However, if an *exclusive* license is requested, meaning you are unable to license the music to anyone else while it's being used for a particular show or film for a period, the sync fee can be substantially higher.

If you are affiliated with a larger music library or publisher, they will handle the negotiations for the type of license and any fees involved. If you are representing yourself, you have the ability to decide what you think is a fair deal for the use of your music.

Buyouts

A *buyout* is when a company offers you a flat license fee for your music that allows them to use it whenever and however they want, forever. A "buyout" also means that you won't make any more money than the license fee from the music, meaning, no performance royalties.

This trend started in the early 2000s with a particular network that shall remain nameless. Instead of licensing music through the "proper" channels, they would find unsigned independent artists via the internet and offer them a $500 buyout for the use of their track. They then proceeded to use that track in almost every different show they produced, all the while not having to pay the artist any royalties.

You may be saying to yourself, "Well, it's a good opportunity for the artist to reach a wider audience." True. But this is a clear-cut example of exploiting an artist using the term "exposure." Most of the artists didn't receive much more than the initial $500.

Buyouts are a predatory way of licensing music. Companies know that most musicians are desperate for any sort of media attention, and they will use that to get an unlimited supply of music for next to nothing.

Buyouts wouldn't be much of an issue if it were only one network doing them. In the last two decades, the trend has been catching on. And more and more musicians are being exploited. I've had buyouts offered to me for commercials, documentaries, and radio spots. You name it, and someone has tried to buy me out. Maybe I'm just an old curmudgeon now, but I've never accepted one, no matter how desperate for cash I may have been at the time.

Another side effect of the buyout is that it has driven way down the licensing fees that composers and artists can receive. It's hard to demand $5,000 for a track when someone else will do it for $500.

However, should you choose to accept a buyout for your music, make sure that it's a *nonexclusive* license. This way you will still have an opportunity to license the same piece of music elsewhere.

There is one type of music that relies entirely on the composer accepting a buyout, and that is music for video games.

Video Games

Video games now generate more revenue than the movie and music industries combined. Because of this, major game developers are able to hire big-name Hollywood composers to score their games.

Game music is like film music in that its job is to create mood and atmosphere for the player/viewer. The key difference between the two is that film music is considered *linear*, meaning it goes from point A to point B and will always be the same, whereas game music is considered *adaptive*. Adaptive music will change and evolve based on the game player's choices. In order to achieve effective results, the composer should think outside the box a bit in how they approach scoring a game.

Skills Required

Along with the necessary skills needed to score a film, there are a few additional skills required for creating effective game music.

- The ability to create seamless loops

- Horizontal resequencing

- Vertical layering

- Familiarity with middleware like FMOD or Wwise

Looping

Creating beds of music that loop seamlessly is an essential part of game music. Because the player can take as much or as little time as they choose to get through a section of a game, the music needs to continue seamlessly throughout the playthrough. Any stops or starts in the music will affect the *immersion* of the player.

Creating a music loop that is seamless is a necessary skill for video game music. It can be as short as few seconds or as long as five minutes. But it must be able to loop around onto itself with no audible clicks or pops. Again, you don't want to do anything that will disrupt the players immersion into the game world, and loops that jump or stutter will definitely do that.

In order to get a loop to repeat seamlessly, you need to make sure that it starts and stops on a *zero-crossing* within its waveform. There are a lot of great tutorials online to help you learn to create these types of loops. And if music for games interests you, this is one skill you will need to master.

Horizontal Resequencing

Once you've mastered the art of creating a seamless loop, the next step is to understand *horizontal resequencing*. Creating one loop for an entire game isn't enough. Each level or area within the game may well require a new music loop.

For instance, if the player moves from one area of the game to another, the music should change—seamlessly. In order for this to happen, the programmers of the game will create a *trigger* that will cause the next loop to start. There may be one loop of music as a player moves through a cave, then they flip a switch that opens a secret door. Flipping the switch could be the trigger that starts the next loop of music.

In order to make the transition from one loop to another seamless, it's important that factors like the tempo and the key remain relatively close to one another. Too big of a shift between loops, again, will cause the players' "immersion" to suffer.

You can practice this by creating two separate eight-bar loops that have different levels of intensity. The first loop may have no discernable rhythmic elements, while the second one has a layer of drums and percussion to ramp up the intensity. The solution is to try not to change the key or tempo; rather, change the dynamic between the loops.

Vertical Layering

The other method of getting the music to adapt to the players' choices in a game is called *vertical layering*. Vertical layering is when you start with an initial loop and as the player interacts and moves around the environment of the game, other loops come in and out, creating different layers of intensity.

For example, you could start with an ambient synth pad that's very atmospheric. As the player wanders into a more dangerous area with enemies lurking about, another loop of tense strings could be triggered and combined with the original ambient layer. Further still, the enemy spots the player. A new loop is added to the existing two that adds a pulsing synth, ramping up the tension. And finally, when the player initiates combat, a loop with pounding percussion enters, adding to the intensity.

The key with vertical layering is that each individual loop should work on its own or any combination of loops can work together to create varying layers of intensity. The programmers of the game determine what action triggers which layer.

This is a very different way of music scoring, and it's a challenge. However, it's a lot of fun to create one piece of music that can do so many different things.

Middleware

Middleware is the software used to implement the changes in audio that happen within a game. The aforementioned triggers are created within the middleware programs.

There are two main middleware systems in use for games, namely, FMOD and Wwise.

The good news for the composer is that you will probably not be responsible for implementing the audio into the game using this software.

Most game studios have an audio director that will handle any implementation, so rest easy.

However, if you're really interested in getting into music for games, you can download either FMOD or Wwise for free and see how they work. Even though you won't be required to implement the audio, knowing how these systems work could give you an advantage over someone who doesn't.

Finding Gigs as a Games Composer

Like everything else, finding a gig as a composer for video games will require you to get in front of the people that could use you, namely, game developers.

Music for games runs the gamut from small low/no budget indie developers all the way up to the AAA-rated, multimillion dollar companies like EA (Electronic Arts) and Ubisoft. Smaller companies are more likely to give a newbie composer a shot, so finding these developers should become a priority.

There are multiple conferences happening every year for game developers, and if you're serious about music for games, it's to your benefit to attend as many as you can. This could get expensive, but it is a business expense. The opportunity to be around hundreds of game developers at the same time outweighs the cost.

There are local game developer conferences, all the way up to the big ones like E3 in Los Angeles or GDC (Game Developers Conference) in San Francisco. Pick a conference, make sure you have your marketing material and a way for the developers to connect with you, and get networking.

Another avenue to approach would be a local college. Like film students, most colleges have some sort of computer programming department. And I'll bet that there are a few aspiring game developers taking some of those classes. Reach out to your local schools to see if they offer any type of game development classes or seminars, and figure out how you can attend them or at least get in touch with the students.

One last, but effective, place to look is online. There are hundreds of game developer forums on the internet. You can join them and offer your services as a composer. There may not be any money involved, but getting your feet wet with the technical specifications required for game music can be worth it.

A lot of game developers also hold what's known as a *game jam*. Game jams are when a group of developers create a working, playable game over the course of a weekend. If you can get involved in these, you can get a lot of experience writing music for different developers. Sometimes, the jams are online; other times, developers will meet up in person.

The more you get out there in front of developers, the more they'll remember you. This is the good type of experience you should be going after.

Pay for Game Music

The pay you can expect for game music is similar to what you can expect for film music. Games usually work with all-in budgets. Because games can sometimes take years to develop and the music may need to be changed or updated as time goes on, a lot of developers will add *milestones* for the budget as well.

Figuring out what to charge will be dependent upon how much music is required. Like a film, you are likely to have some form of a spotting session with the game's director to discuss when and where music needs to be. Unlike a film, a game may consist of many hours of original music, all adaptable, so it's important for you to figure out how much time and effort the job may take you.

For games, apply the same calculation you used to figure out the cost per minute of music for a film. This will give you a good frame of reference for what you should be aiming for as far as your fee goes.

As mentioned earlier, music for games is typically a buyout, meaning you won't make any royalties on the music you create for the game. This is standard for most games; the only exception to this rule is if you're someone like Hans Zimmer. (Are you Hans Zimmer? If so, hi!)

If the game company decides to release the soundtrack of the game, you may have a bit of negotiating power, but make sure you read any agreement before you sign it. And if you don't understand something, ask or take it to a lawyer. You don't have to sign something you don't understand.

MEDIA COMPOSER CHECKLIST

Project Information

Project Title: _____   Delivery Date: _____

Director: _____   Contact Info: _____

No. of Cues: _____   Est. Minutes of Music: _____

Cost per Minute of Music: _____   Est. Total Composer Fee:_____

Project Genre:_____   Project Mood: _____

Instrumentation: _____

_____

Live Musicians: _____Yes/No_____   Musician Rate: _____

Composer Checklist

☐ Rough Cut?   ☐ SMPTE Start Point?   ☐ Frame Rate?

☐ Mock-Up?   ☐ Bit Depth/Sample Rate?   ☐ File Delivery?

Additional Spotting Session Notes

_____

_____

_____

_____

_____

_____

_____

_____

Figure 7.1. Media Composer Checklist
Author

Teaching Gigs

For a musician, teaching is usually the quickest way to start creating a steady income stream. If you understand the basics of whatever it is that you do, chances are there is someone who could benefit from your knowledge.

I got my first gig as a teacher at a local music store when I was eighteen years old. I was a bit nervous at first to take the job primarily because I was saying to myself, "Why should anyone listen to me? I'm only eighteen. What do I know?"

When I sat down with my first student and realized that they were a complete beginner, my fears subsided. I realized all I had to do was show them where to put their hands and how to count basic rhythms, and they were happy to have the information.

I realized that even though I didn't know everything, I knew enough to give my students something on which to work that would help them progress. And that was all they really wanted.

As time went on, I started developing a method of teaching that was so successful with my students, that by the end of my first year as a teacher, I had around sixty students a week—at $30 per hour. I was making fairly good money for an eighteen-year-old. Because most of my lessons were during the day, I had time at night to pursue all of my cover band gigs, where I made even more money!

The point is, teaching can be a great way to supplement your income as a musician. You also get the added bonus of helping others get into music as well. The only drawback to teaching is "the trap."

"The Trap"

There's a saying that floats around the music industry, "Those that can't do—teach." Unfortunately, there is a bit of truth to this.

I've been extremely fortunate to have teachers who actually worked at the thing that they taught. However, I've also had teachers who taught how to do things from a purely *theoretical* standpoint.

When I was in college, I landed a gig playing for a dinner theater. We were doing the show *The Best Little Whorehouse in Texas*, which required me to break out my Telecaster and play a bunch of country licks all night. The gig paid about $1,200 a week. Not bad.

One day in my private lesson with my guitar instructor at the college, he asked me, "Are you playing around town at all?" to which I replied, "Yeah, I got this great little gig playing country licks." He looked at me in all seriousness and said, "You need to quit playing that country shit; it's hurting your jazz chops." I was perplexed. I was going to college to become a professional musician, yet here was my teacher telling me to stop playing a well-paying gig because it wasn't jazz. In that moment, I realized that he was in "the trap."

"The trap" is when you get so comfortable teaching that you actually stop doing the thing that it is that you teach. My college instructor was a tenured professor; he didn't need to worry about going out and making a living as an actual working musician anymore. He was comfortable.

Don't get me wrong; there are those whose desire is only to teach, and they study and go to school to earn that right. If that's your desire, then go for it.

For me though, my greatest successes as a teacher have come from relaying my experiences as a working professional to my students.

At times, I, too, have almost fallen into the trap. Finding a balance between actually doing the thing that you teach and teaching it is imperative if you want to be effective as a teacher for anything creative.

Skills Needed

- The Three Core Skills: technical proficiency, a great ear, and the ability to communicate effectively

- Patience

- A desire to constantly evolve and change as the industry changes

As a teacher you need to have a developed knowledge of the techniques required to do the thing that you teach. And you should have a good theoretical understanding of the subject.

You should possess the ability to articulate ideas in a way that is easy for your students to understand. Think of the saying, "Show me as if I were a two-year-old."

Most of all, patience is a necessity. Even though you understand the subject, not every student will comprehend the information the same way. You may have to work harder with some students than others, so never lose your patience with a student.

> *For me though, my greatest successes as a teacher have come from relaying my experiences as a working professional to my students.*

Where to Find Potential Students

Like all the other gigs discussed here, finding students is all about getting them to know you exist.

Printing up a flyer offering lessons and posting at the various music stores in town is a great way to target some potential students. Make sure you put the subject that you are offering to teach in big bold letters and include a way for the potential students to contact you—phone, email, QR code, and so on.

Other places you could place flyers around town would be venues where they have live music—a coffee shop, a local club, a community center, or places of worship. Schools are another option, from elementary to the local college. Make sure you get permission from the school administrators before you post any flyers, as they can be very particular as to whom they let on campus.

Another option is the internet. You could post an ad on Craigslist offering your teaching services. Join a Facebook group of local musicians and post an ad in the forums. Instagram, Twitter, and LinkedIn are all viable options that provide great visibility.

One of the ways I ramped up my private student count was to offer one free lesson to new students. In the free lesson, I'd show them something really cool to get them excited, and then they would sign up for more (hopefully).

Get creative with your marketing. Try to show potential students why they should study with you, instead of someone else.

Teaching Private Students

The most common type of music lesson is the private lesson. The benefit of private students is that the student gets a more personalized lesson experience. They can go at their own pace without feeling like they're falling behind another student. You can also tailor the lessons to their strengths and weaknesses.

If you're teaching out of your house, make sure you have everything necessary to conduct the lesson as smoothly as possible—music stands, some sort of playback device so the student can play along, cables if they need to plug in their instrument, a metronome, a comfortable chair for both you and the student, extra strings, picks, reeds, or rosin, whatever you may need to keep the lesson up and running.

Along with any equipment you may need, make sure your house is clean. I can't stress this point enough. No one wants to come back for another lesson if your place is gross. If you own pets, keep them cordoned off while teaching. Some of your students may either be afraid of certain animals or, worse, allergic. So keep this in mind.

If you're teaching younger children out of your personal residence, chances are the student's parents may be hesitant about leaving them alone in a "stranger's" house. This is normal; while I never allow the parents to sit and watch the lesson (it can make both the student and the teacher nervous, rendering the lesson ineffective), I always provided a place for them to hang out during the lesson, normally in a different room. I'd also set out snacks and drinks so they could be comfortable while they waited.

The other option for teaching privately is going to a student's house and setting the lesson up there. If this is the case, make sure you're able to bring all the necessary equipment to provide an effective lesson. This may take some creativity on your part to make everything portable.

If traveling to your students, you'll also take into account travel time and traffic. This should also factor into the rate you charge as well. If the student is coming to you, it's easy to do back-to-back students. If you have to travel from one place to another, it will cut into the number of hours you are able to teach in a given day, therefore cutting your earning potential. So adjust accordingly.

Teaching Private Lessons for a Music School or Music Store

The benefits of teaching at a private music school or local music store are that the students and teachers show up at one neutral location. Most music schools and stores that offer lessons have private lesson rooms that come equipped with all the necessary equipment to conduct an effective lesson.

This is a great option if you're not into the idea of your students coming to your house or having to drive around town to your students' houses to conduct lessons.

Being brought on board as a teacher at a private music school may require you to have at minimum an associate degree in the subject you teach and submit a résumé and be interviewed.

Teaching at a local music store can be a bit easier to get into. You may still have to provide a résumé, but the criteria to be brought on board as a teacher won't be as strict.

The upside of teaching at one of these types of places is that the students, most likely, will be brought to you. The downside is that you won't have much control over what you charge per lesson. While you can try to negotiate what you want per lesson, most schools and stores have a standard lesson rate that won't be changed. They will also take a percentage of your lesson income as "rent" for use of the lesson space.

For a short time, I worked for a small, private music school here in LA. I was getting paid around $45 per lesson, which I thought was fine, until I learned that the school was charging the students around $75 per lesson. Once I learned that I was missing out on an extra $30 per lesson, I didn't hang around much longer. However, this is the case with most music schools. They have to pay for their overhead and will upcharge the students for the lessons while paying you less. I bring this up just so you're aware that this can happen—don't be surprised.

Teaching Online

Online lessons have been around for a while now. However, since the COVID-19 pandemic, many teachers have migrated to online lessons.

Teaching online via Zoom or Skype allows you to connect with students that may not live in your immediate area. Therefore, it offers opportunities to grow your student base beyond your normal geographic area.

Acquiring online students involves a bit of savvier marketing on your end than just posting some flyers. If it is your desire to teach online, you will absolutely need a website. Your website will allow you to connect with your students, accept payment, schedule lesson times, and provide any materials that may be required.

One way of targeting potential students is to buy an ad on Google or YouTube and target it to people interested in whatever instrument or subject you're teaching. These ads can be expensive, but the reach they have can be worth the cost.

Teaching online also requires you to be a bit more technologically inclined than teaching in person. Whichever platform you decide to use, you will want to make sure there is a screen-share feature as well as the ability to share your computer's audio. I've been using Zoom for my online lessons because at this moment, it offers the best options for both video and audio.

Because you're teaching music in an online format, it's vital that the audio you are providing from your end is top notch. Don't rely on the microphone in your computer to capture what you're doing. You will need to invest in some sort of audio interface and an external microphone to get the best possible sound. Fortunately, you don't have to spend an arm and a leg on either of these devices, but having even a less expensive setup will be better than nothing.

Because I teach music production and mixing in an online format, I've also invested in special software that allows for high-quality stereo audio to be passed through my computer to the student. Rogue Amoeba's Loopback is a great way to route the audio from your computer directly to your online meetings.

Making sure that the student is receiving the best quality audio from your end will help justify the cost of the lesson. So don't overlook the importance of this.

There are also some websites like www.lessonface.com, www.takeles sons.com, and www.schoolofrock.com that allow most anyone to sign up as a teacher and create a profile. You can even set your rates on some sites. These sites work as if you are teaching in a music store. They will handle the marketing and search for students; in return, you will pay them a piece of your overall fee for the service.

The Pay for Private Lessons

The easiest way to charge students is by the hour. Use the Hourly Rate Calculator to figure out your minimum hourly rate and adjust from there (see Chapter 3).

Because lessons typically occur once a week at a certain time, I charge the students by the month. If the students lesson is on Tuesdays at 3:00 and there are four Tuesdays in the month, I would have them pay me four times the hourly rate at the beginning of the month. This is to lock them into my schedule and encourage them to show up. The problem with charging as you go is that the student may decide that they don't want to have a lesson that day. However, you have them scheduled and have reserved that time slot for them. If they don't show, you lose the chance of scheduling another student in that time slot.

Charging by the month for lessons keeps everyone honest. It lets the students know that you are committing your time to them, and they'll most likely show up because they've paid in advance for the lesson.

You should also adopt a strict cancellation policy. I allow for a twenty-four-hour window to cancel a lesson with no penalty. If a student can't make their scheduled lesson time, they have to let me know at least twenty-four hours before they're scheduled to show up. I won't refund their money, but I will reschedule the lesson. If the student tries to cancel within the twenty-four-hour window, I won't reschedule, and they will lose the money that they paid for the time. The only time I ever make an exception to this is when the student has some sort of emergency and it can't be avoided. "Billy has a soccer game" isn't an emergency; "Billy's grandma is in the hospital" is.

The flip side of this would be if you have to cancel the lesson for some reason. If you know you'll be out of town for part of the month, let the student know and don't charge them for the time you'll be away.

If you have to cancel a student last minute due to an emergency, offer to make up the lesson at another time or prorate it to the next month. Remember, your students' time is just as valuable as yours. And showing respect to your students in this way will keep them coming back for more lessons.

Teaching at an Accredited School

Most public schools (elementary, high school) and universities require you to have a degree of some sort in order to teach there. The exception to this rule is that some schools have adjunct instructors that teach a specific subject and have extensive real-world experience in a particular field that can bypass the accreditation rules of the state.

If it is your desire to teach at one of these types of schools, I recommend getting at least a bachelor's degree before you apply.

If your lifelong ambition is to teach music professionally full time, I applaud you for that. However, be careful of "the trap." If you want to be effective teaching a creative subject, it's imperative that you continue to be creative with the tools that you teach to your students.

My success as a teacher is due to the fact that I continue to work professionally in the area in which I teach. This allows me to connect my real-world experience with the theoretical lessons I give to my students. This helps bridge the gap between "book smart" and "street smart."

I was the type of student that needed to see how the ideas being taught to me were relevant to the work I would be doing later in life. And the teachers that were able to show me the *why* as opposed to just the *what* were the ones from whom I learned the most.

Most accredited schools also have a set of procedures for curriculum development, attendance taking, quizzes, and testing protocols, so become familiar with the way a particular school does things before you start.

Getting a Gig at an Accredited School

If you have a degree or equivalent real-world experience, finding openings at a school is relatively easy.

Most schools post openings for teaching positions on their websites. Scroll through and see if the subject you teach has an opening. The school will list the requirements for the position within the posting. Make sure you fit the criteria before applying.

Schools sometimes post any openings they have on certain social media sites like LinkedIn or www.indeed.com.

Do a quick search of your area; you may be surprised how many options may be available to you.

The Pay for Accredited Schools

The pay you will get teaching at an accredited school can either be hourly or salary. In your initial interview, you may be asked what you would like to be paid, or they may tell you what the position pays beforehand.

If the position is hourly, figure your baseline hourly rate and adjust it to where you're comfortable.

If it's a salaried position and they ask what you would like for a salary, take your hourly rate and multiply it by a forty-hour workweek. There's your salary. Be sure to check that your paid hours include grading homework and faculty meetings.

The pay will depend on either the type of degree that you hold or your relevant work experience.

One thing about teaching at an accredited school that is different than most other situations a working musician encounters is that these schools may offer some sort of benefits! Of course, these are dependent upon the number of hours you work.

Health, dental, paid vacations, or 401(k)'s are really worth their weight in gold to a musician. The only time in my life that I was offered these perks was when I took the gig at the Musicians Institute College of Contemporary Music in Hollywood.

Because benefits are so valuable, being offered them can sometimes offset a salary that is lower than you may have anticipated. In the end, it's up to you to decide what your time is worth.

One piece of advice that I will give you: If offered the option to contribute to a 401(k) as part of your deal, take it. Most workplaces will match a percentage of your 401(k) contribution. I've seen as much as 6%. It's basically free money that will grow exponentially over time (see Chapter 9).

TEACHING CHECKLIST

Student Information

Student Name:_____   Contact Info: _____

Lesson Day/Time: _____   Lesson Rate: _____

Lesson Location: _____   Address: _____

Student Goals: _____

Current Level of Proficiency: _____

Lesson Checklist

☐ Instrument   ☐ Amplification?   ☐ Playback Device

☐ Cables   ☐ Lesson Materials   ☐ Music Stand

☐ Instrument Accessories   ☐ Payment Schedule?

Additional Student Requests

_____

_____

_____

_____

_____

_____

_____

_____

_____

_____

Figure 7.2.   Teaching Checklist
Author

Conclusion

At some point in my career, I've done every type of gig listed. I know this isn't everything available, but from these different types of gigs you may find other opportunities arise. It's important to always keep your eyes (and ears) open for new opportunities. There really is no telling where a gig may pop up and surprise you.

FAILURE AND HOW TO PICK YOURSELF UP

Malte Mueller/Getty Images

At the time of this writing, we are going through a very strange time culturally. There seems to be a zero-sum mentality where if you are not "winning," you are "losing." There is no in between. This is a very dangerous mindset to have; life is not black and white. Failure or "losing" is part of the journey. It's how we learn and grow from our mistakes. Failure is how we learn who we are and what limitations we possess. Failure is how we strengthen our resolve and pull ourselves back from the brink. The only way to fully fail at becoming a professional musician is to quit altogether. Aside from that, there is always hope no matter how dark it may seem.

Failure can be a catalyst that sets you off in a new direction that you may not have seen before. A door opens that was previously closed. My entire career has been fraught with failures. It still continues to this day. The concept that you must grasp is that *when you do fail, you must learn from that failure.* Something didn't work this time needs to be adjusted. If you don't learn from your mistakes and continue to persist in whatever caused you to fail, don't expect a different result. They say the definition of insanity is doing the same thing over and over again and expecting a different result.

Sometimes, you won't be able to identify where you went wrong; sometimes, it has nothing at all to do with your actions.

When I arrived in Los Angeles, I did a ton of auditions for touring artists. At most of them, the music director hired me on the spot, only to fire me the next day for some asinine reason. For instance, I was literally given the excuse that I was too tall and made the 5'1" singer look too small when I stood next to her. I took the firings personally, like something was wrong with me.

The situation was completely beyond my control. There's nothing that I could have done to change the outcome of this, save for physically altering my height.

This taught me a very important lesson. Sometimes, shit happens. Yes, it was a stupid excuse for being fired, but getting upset over it serves no purpose other than to make me feel inadequate. I had to learn to separate myself from my craft. Sometimes, it's just not the right gig, so you move on to the next.

This mindset really helped me out when I started pitching my music for licensing. I used to take it personally when someone rejected one of my songs. Then, I realized that my song is fine, but it wasn't a good fit for this particular project. When I licensed the same song a few months later, this theory was proven correct.

If I were to put a percentage on how many of my endeavors are successful, I would say it's around 5%. That means that 95% of the time I'm dealing with rejection. As a younger man, I probably would have given up by now. However, having persisted for two decades in these small failures, I know that if I ever stop, it would be the ultimate failure.

Robert Fripp from the band King Crimson has a quote that I read when I was around nineteen years old that has always stuck with me. He says, "There are no mistakes, save one: the failure to learn from a mistake."

So there you have it. No matter what level you're at, you're going to deal with failure. It's a constant cycle. Even as you rise in the ranks, there will be occurrences that will try to throw you off your game. You must persist, adapt, and move forward. Even if you have to take a step back for a minute, as long as you persist, you will overcome your hurdles and encounter success.

Napoleon Hill

Forewarning here—I am trying to be a reasonable advocate of artists fulfilling their dreams of becoming professional musicians and making a living at it. What I am about to write may be considered reckless or irresponsible in the eyes of some. Take what is said here, digest it, think long and hard about it, and make your own decision on what's best for you.

When I was eighteen years old, my mom gave me a copy of Napoleon Hill's Think and Grow Rich. *I read it. I thought it was pretty good, but nothing really hit me or changed the way I was going about things. It wasn't until I was older, when I took another look at it, that I realized I missed some very important things.*

If you don't know about this book, it was written in 1937. So there are some things that may not be considered PC these days, but there is a wealth of good information that still holds true today.

The author is trying to figure out why some people are super successful and others are not. He tries to find a common trait that all successful people seem to possess, and in my opinion, he absolutely nails it. I highly recommend you check it out. It may take a few reads for it to sink in, but it's worth it.

The two most important things I took away from this book are what I want to discuss as follows.

Plan B

One common trait that Napoleon Hill discovered about successful people is that they tend to be laser focused on what they want to achieve. That being said, there is no other option than succeeding at what they want, no backup plan—it's success or bust.

When you are a child, you are taught that anything is possible and to dream big. But somewhere during your upbringing, you are told the dreams of your youth may not be the most responsible plans for your future. Case in point, how many of you have told a parent or loved one that you want to go to school for something you love or to pursue a passion you've had all your life and be met with, "Well, that's great, but just make sure you have a backup plan if things don't work out for you."

Understand that when someone suggests you have a safety net, it's most likely coming from a place of love and genuine concern about your future. That's a good thing. Be happy you have someone that cares enough for your well-being to discuss these things with you.

Here's the problem, though, with backup plans: You know what it is that you want out of your life and career and begin to pursue it. However, all the while in the back of your mind, you tell yourself that if this doesn't work, you could always do "this" instead. It's this mindset that's going to hinder your progress with the thing that you actually want to do.

It's like having one foot planted in your safe zone while trying to move forward. If one foot is planted, it's going to severely limit your forward momentum. You may not commit fully to the things that are necessary to succeed because in the back of your mind, you have a way out if things get too tough.

To paraphrase a story that Napoleon Hill sums up fairly well:

"There's this general in ancient Greece. His city is under siege by the enemy; they are outnumbered, underequipped. The general knows his chances are slim, so he decides to do something bold. He orders his soldiers to get on the boats in the harbor, tells them to sail around behind the invaders, and land them on the beach with the invaders in front of them. The general has his soldiers disembark onto the beach and then turns to the boats' captains and orders them to burn the boats to the ground, effectively leaving his army with an ocean behind them and an army in front of them—no escape.

He tells the soldiers that they have a choice: Fight like they have nothing left to lose or lay down and die on this beach."

It's a very harsh tactic to use, but highly effective. The general has removed any chance for his soldiers to back out of this situation. Face it, head on, or quit.

If you give yourself a way out. Chances are you will take it at the first sign of things getting tough. I can't tell you how many people I've seen come and go in the two decades I've been in LA. People come here, encounter a bit of resistance, and then head back to their hometown where things are safe.

I am *not* telling you to give up on your responsibilities or your current day job to pursue your dreams right now. But at some point, you will have to make a choice for yourself and burn your boats to commit fully to the thing that you want to do. You will know then the time is right.

Persistence

The second trait that Napoleon Hill noticed about successful people is that they don't quit, no matter what adversity they face.

He sums it up in another story that I feel is appropriate:

"This story is about an investment banker who decided to quit his nice, safe job and head West to strike it rich during the gold rush.

The banker quits his job, sells his possessions, and fully commits to the idea of becoming a successful prospector.

He is following the idea of the Greek general, burning his boats, no backup plan; it's this or nothing.

The banker purchases a large plot of land and sets out to fulfill his dreams of striking it rich. Within a few weeks his plan pays off, and he pulls around three to four million dollars' worth of gold from his land. We're talking mid-1800s money, so adjusted for inflation, it's a lot!

The banker feels vindicated in his decision to just go for it and decides to reinvest the majority of his findings in more equipment and workers to continue mining his property.

For nearly two years, they dig, and they dig, but they find nothing. He starts to panic. The initial money he had made is almost gone. He eventually breaks down and sells his land with all the mining equipment for pennies on the dollar.

The man he sells the property to comes in with a geological surveyor to map out the property. While perusing the property, the surveyor notices where the mining was taking place and realized that they were digging in the wrong area. If they moved the equipment three feet over, there is a chance that they may find something.

The new owner decides to give it a shot, fires up the equipment, and begins to dig where the surveyor suggested. Lo and behold, they find one of the largest gold deposits in Colorado history."

The point of this story is persistence in the face of adversity. It's all well and good to go full bore at what you want with no backup plan, but know that it won't be easy. There will always be things that show up and try to knock you off your path. What's been discussed about failure applies here.

Another favorite author of mine is Steven Pressfield, who wrote a book titled *The War of Art*. In the book, he calls these problems encountered on your journey "resistance." And the only way to deal with resistance is to continue pushing forward, no matter what.

Resistance comes in many forms. You may be humming along having some success, when all of a sudden, *BAM*, your car breaks down so that the money you were saving to buy some new gear is gone.

Resistance can be anything that tries to keep you from achieving your goal. When these things happen, it's easy to want to just curl up and quit.

> *"At many times in my life, I have questioned if I made the right decision to continue pursuing music. However, because I had nothing else to fall back on, I had to persevere or do nothing."*

Without taking a chance on the things that we want to do, we are guaranteed to never achieve them. If doing what you love was easy, everyone would be doing it.

The universe likes to test your resolve. Some of my greatest achievements came directly after some of my greatest failures. So persevere. Push through those dark times, and as comedian Steve Harvey says, "Your parachute will open, but you have to jump first. If you don't jump, one thing is for sure, you'll be safe, but you'll never soar."

Ego

Your ego can be your best friend and your worst enemy. As musicians, we all have some degree of it. Knowing when to check it is paramount in maintaining success in this business.

Confidence vs. Arrogance

What's the difference? Confidence and arrogance look very similar on the surface, and they can seem almost interchangeable; however, that couldn't be further from the truth.

In order to succeed in anything, you need to have confidence in your abilities that you can do the tasks assigned to you. You need to know yourself well enough to promote your strengths to others, while being fully aware of your weaknesses. Without this self-awareness, you may overcompensate for your weaknesses just to take a gig. I can guarantee one thing will happen; eventually you will be found out. If may take some time, but eventually your weaknesses will show themselves and damage your reputation.

So know what you can and can't do. Once you know your limitations, you can then work on those weak points. But you have to be honest with yourself first.

An arrogant person won't acknowledge any weakness, either to themselves or to others. They tend to just bulldoze their way to whatever it is they're going after, regardless of whom they crush in their path. I've worked with a lot of "successful" arrogant people. I say "successful" because, in the industry's eyes, they were highly sought after. Over time, however, these individuals' weaknesses started to show, and most are now shunned by the same industry professionals that once praised them.

The easiest way you can spot whether or not you're dealing with a confident or arrogant person is this: An arrogant person works for their own ego. They can't accept criticism; they will shoot down good ideas because they feel threatened by them.

A confident person works for the greater good of the project. They are willing to accept criticism when it's warranted. They are open to any ideas that will make the endeavor more successful.

Pros vs. Amateurs

The same kind of assessment can be used to determine whether you're dealing with a pro or an amateur. Or if you are presenting yourself as one or the other.

Pros are always going to be supportive of others' endeavors. If they have a critique to give, it's in the spirit of building, as opposed to tearing down. One thing a pro never does is talk shit about another's work. They understand that it takes a lot of courage to put yourself out there. If they don't have anything nice to say, they say nothing. If asked about something they don't like, they can always find the good in any project and highlight that.

An amateur is the complete opposite. They are swirling in negativity. They revel in tearing down the work and successes of others. The old guitar player joke that goes "How many guitarists does it take to change a light bulb? Seven. One to change it and the other six to stand around with their arms folded talking about how they could have changed it better," sums up the amateur mentality.

Therefore, you need to ask yourself this: Are you a pro, or are you an amateur?

Criticism

Whether giving or taking, criticism is a part of life as a musician. Once again, you have to ask yourself where it's coming from. Is it from a constructive place or is it meant to tear down? Once you determine the criticism's origin, it makes it easy to either take it to heart or brush it off as nothing of consequence.

If someone is genuinely trying to help, accept it; don't get hurt over it. See if they're on to something. They just might be. This is an excellent way of progressing as an artist.

If you know it's coming from someone's ego, pay no mind to it. There are those in this world who revel in their ability to tear others down. They do this because it makes them feel good about themselves. The real root of this is that they feel small on the inside, and if they tear others down to their level, they feel like they have some control over their miserable lives. Never let them get the better of you.

If you know yourself well enough, you will be able to navigate the treacherous waters of the ego-driven sociopaths with relative ease.

MANAGING YOUR FINANCES

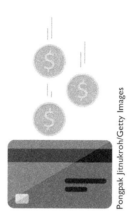

Pongpak Jitnukroh/Getty Images

O nce you've gone through all the necessary steps to establish your-self as a professional musician, the next hurdle you will face is maintaining and conserving the money you have started to make. As discussed earlier, sustainability is the biggest issue you face as a working professional. It can be nerve-racking to make really good money one month and then make nothing for the next three.

You will need to learn to manage your finances in a way that antici-pates these downtimes. In the beginning, this can be the most difficult task at hand. But even as you move through your career, it's a good habit to get into the routine of anticipating downtime. You don't want to find yourself faced with a mountain of expenses and no money to take care of them.

However, with a little planning and discipline you'll be all right.

Saving

It's a good idea to start setting aside a certain percentage of your income from every gig you take. Pretend that you are making 30% less that what you actually earn, for two reasons: one is anticipating that you will have to pay taxes, and the other is sustainability.

Remember that because you are independent now, you are responsible for those taxes. It can be a devastating thing to get an enormous tax bill at the end of the year and not be able to pay it. The other reason to set aside income is for the leaner times. Try to set yourself up to have at least six months of expenses saved at any given moment. This doesn't mean that you're going to take a six-month vacation. It means that if work gets slow, you'll be covered and have a bit of a cushion to go out and hustle up some more work.

In the beginning, not everyone is going to have the luxury of a six-month cushion, but this is something that you should always keep in mind. Even if you're working a lot right now, start thinking that the gig could go away tomorrow and ask yourself, "Will I be okay? And for how long?"

Start by setting up a savings account and put away whatever you comfortably can for that rainy day that will eventually show up. Obviously, the more you set aside, the more comfortable of a cushion you will have for yourself. But at least, start with any amount that's left over after your expenses.

Set a Budget (and Stick to It)

It may be tempting to buy that new piece of gear or that really nice guitar you saw in the store. You may feel that if you just get that new mic preamp, it will solve all your problems.

Before you start spending all the money you've earned, however, make sure there's room in the budget. You have to have an honest approach when looking at your finances. Don't kid yourself about what you can and can't really afford. Add up all of your expenses, and write them down. Figure out how much you need to cover everything. (Remember, this is how you figured your hourly rate.) This tells you what you need to target for every month. Knowing how much you require every month will help you when making purchasing decisions. Never buy anything outside of your monthly budget until you know that you have made enough to cover all of the necessities. Even if you do make more money than you actually need for the month, scrutinize every extraneous purchase. Ask yourself, "Do I really need this?"

If there is something that you really want and it exceeds your budget, start saving for it by adding it to the next monthly budget. That way it becomes part of your expenses and you can adjust accordingly.

You should also allocate a portion of your budget for recreational things—movies, concerts, and going out with friends.

Remember, being an artist requires you to experience life so that you have something to say. Make sure you don't forget to go and experience things; it'll make your songs better!

Credit

Credit, I have found, is one of the most misunderstood aspects of our culture. At no point in my schooling did anyone explain what it was and why it's important.

Credit exists as a system of "trust" between you and a financial lender. Your credit score shows the lender how "trustworthy" you are when they're deciding to lend you money. You need credit for expensive things like houses and cars, which most people don't have the actual cash on hand to pay for.

Maintaining a good credit score is critical if you ever want to buy your own house, a reliable car, or new gear. It will affect how much you can borrow and how much interest you will pay. The higher your score, the more you can borrow, and usually at a lower interest rate.

Ignoring your credit score can have devastating consequences. Even if you know that you've messed up, it's important to get honest with yourself about where you stand. If you've never had a credit card or applied for credit, you may feel that you are in good standing. This couldn't be further from the truth.

Checking Your Credit

I avoided credit cards for years, and always paid for everything in cash. I thought this was a good and responsible thing and that my credit rating would be okay. Imagine my shock when I couldn't get a cell phone contract without paying a huge deposit. I realized I needed to get better acquainted with my credit situation if I wanted to be able to function as a responsible "adult."

The first thing you can do to get a grasp on where you stand is to get your three credit reports. Yes, I said three. There are three credit reporting agencies: Equifax, TransUnion, and Experian. You need to look at all of them. Fortunately, you are able to pull all three credit reports for free once a year at www.annualcreditreport.com.

You will have to sign in, provide your social security number, and answer some broad security questions. However, once you're in, you can download your three reports.

These reports won't have an actual score on them. What they will show you is a detailed financial footprint. You will be able to see things like your car payment history and how often you pay your bills on time. You will also be able to see if there are any "derogatory" marks against you.

Derogatory Marks

If you miss a car payment, default on a credit card, forget to pay your cable bill, they will all be there on your credit report. If things get bad, you may be sent to a collection agency so they can try to recover any money you owe. If you've ever gotten a call from a debt collector, they are not fun. They purposely try to make you feel like a loser and sometimes threaten you if you don't pay up.

Honestly, I still don't answer phone numbers I don't recognize because of this. Even though I don't have any derogatory marks and my credit is fine, the trauma of dealing with debt collectors is still there.

One thing to understand about derogatory marks on your credit is that they stay there for at least seven years. The thing they don't tell you about derogatory marks is that even if you pay them off, they still don't go away. In fact, once you pay off a debt you owe to a collection agency, it actually resets the clock for another seven years. So even if you wait six years to pay it, once it's paid, it will reset for another seven years. It will note that the debt has been paid, but lenders don't care if it was paid or not. All they see is that you messed up, and you may mess up again, which will severely impact how much you can borrow if any.

Cleaning Up Your Credit

You can wait the seven years for the marks to fall off your credit report to start cleaning it up, but this isn't a sound strategy. Here are some things that you can do to start fixing some problems with your credit report right away.

1. Pay it off—As I noted earlier, you can pay off the debts you owe. The problem is that the clock will reset for seven more

years. Your intention is to remove any negative remarks from your report. If you want to pay off the debt, there is a way to do it where the derogatory marks will be removed permanently.

- First, contact the debt collector and tell them you want to settle.

- One thing to remember about debt collectors is that they are normally not the original creditor.

- Debt collection agencies tend to buy people's debt in bulk from certain companies for pennies on the dollar. The original creditor just writes off your debt as a loss for the company. Therefore, you may owe $400, but the collection agency bought your debt for around $0.40 (*no joke!*). If they collect the debt from you, they stand to make a huge profit.

- Knowing this, you have room to negotiate what you owe. Most of the time you can tell them that you can only pay say $100 and ask if they would settle for that. You'd be surprised how quickly they'll jump at an offer like this.

- They may try to wrangle some more money out of you but stay strong.

You're not finished yet. Remember, just because you pay it, doesn't mean it's going to go away. Once the debt collector agrees to settle with you, you need to ask them to send you a letter stating that once the debt is taken care of, it should be removed from your credit report. Don't pay a dime until they agree to this.

2. Dispute—You have the ability to dispute any derogatory marks on your credit report. It's a little involved, but worth it when it works. Here's how you do it:

- Once you've downloaded your three credit reports, check them for any inaccuracies, and then go to each of the credit reports' respective websites. You can use the number at the top of your credit report to sign in and pull up your current report via their website.

- There, you can scroll down to any negative item, and if you hover over it with your mouse, you should get the option to dispute the item. Go ahead and go through whatever process the site asks you to do to file a dispute.

- You should get a conformation that the item has been disputed. One of the things about debt collectors that is misunderstood is that when they buy your debt from a creditor, they normally buy a giant spreadsheet with your name, phone number, original creditor, and how much you owe. Your name will be on a list with hundreds of other debtors. This is all the information they typically have. Why is it important to know this?

- Here's why: When you dispute a derogatory mark with a credit reporting agency, you put the burden of proof on the debt collector to prove that you owe that money, meaning that once you dispute, the debt collector has to prove to the credit reporting agency that you actually owe that money. That means that they have to provide the documentation of the original debt. And because they don't usually have these things on hand, more often than not, the derogatory mark will be removed.

- However, if it comes back that they can prove that you owe the debt, proceed with option one. If you've ever seen signs for a credit repair agency, this is exactly what they do. However, they charge you money to do it. You can try this for yourself; it won't harm your credit if you dispute anything.

3. Judgments—Unfortunately, there are some debt collectors that are very aggressive in their attempts to collect from you. Some may even have an army of lawyers that will sue you for the debt. If this ever happens, you have to act fast. If you receive a subpoena in the mail from a debt collector, it's advisable to hire an attorney, preferably one who deals with debt and collections. Often, these debt collectors will use nefarious means in order to get a judgment against you.

A judgment on your credit report will not be easy to remove and will impact your score dramatically. A judgment will also allow the debt collector to garnish your wages or seize your assets—very serious.

I actually had this happen to me, and it was an absolute nightmare to deal with. I owed $800 for a guitar I bought when I was nineteen years old. I was doing fine with making my payments on time; then I moved and forgot to change my address. This was the time before online bill pay, so the bill would come in the mail and I would mail a check for the payment. I missed a few payments, and with penalties and late fees, I eventually got turned so upside down on what I owed for the guitar that I couldn't make the payments and ended up defaulting on it.

Cut to five years later. I received a notice in the mail that I had had a judgment filed against me for $2,500 from a law firm in New York. I called the number, and they told me that they had sent me a subpoena to show up in court. Because I never received it and didn't show up in court to defend myself, a judge ruled against me and in favor of the debt collector.

Needless to say, I was pretty freaked out. So I did some research into the law firm that sued me. I found out that they were notorious for filing these lawsuits against people and sending the paperwork to the wrong address. Therefore, the ones being sued wouldn't show in court, thus resulting in a default judgment for the debt collector. Shady!

If I had received the subpoena and showed up in court, all I would have had to do was make the debt collector prove that I owed the debt by presenting the original paperwork, just like disputing with the credit reporting agency. The burden of proof would have been on the law firm, not me. Knowing that they wouldn't have had that original information, I would have walked away clean. But because I had a judgment filed in court against me, it was now what's called public record. This allowed the debt collector to aggressively pursue me for the money.

The thing to understand about judgments is that they have a "statute of limitations." This means, depending on your state, that after a certain time period, the debt collector can't come after you anymore unless they file a new lawsuit.

If this ever happens, it's best to handle it immediately. A judgment can get out of hand very quickly. My $800 guitar payment ballooned to over $13,000! If you can't afford to pay off the debt, get on a payment plan. You can still negotiate when you have a judgment, and always ask for written proof that the debt is paid and will not be reported to the credit agencies anymore.

Vigilant monitoring of your credit can help you avoid any scary surprises, so make sure to check it on a regular basis.

Credit Scores

A credit score is a number that corresponds to your financial "trustworthiness." It ranges from 300–850, with 300 obviously being terrible and 850 considered perfect credit. The average credit score lands normally somewhere between 600 and 750. As I said before, just pulling your credit reports won't show you your actual numerical score. To find out your actual number, you may have to sign up with a credit monitoring service. There are some free ones like creditkarma.com. It will show you your TransUnion and Equifax scores. If you sign up for certain credit cards, they may come with a credit score monitor. Browse around, but be wary about giving out your social security number to a site or a person you don't know or trust.

There are many factors that make up your overall score. The things that will impact your score the most will be payment history and derogatory marks. As long as you make all of your payments on time, you'll be fine. It's recommended to set up autopay for recurring bills; that way you will be guaranteed to never miss a payment or be late. As long as you keep this up, your score will gradually begin to rise. One derogatory mark, however, will cause your score to nosedive, sometimes as much as 100 points. So if they show up, take care of those as soon as you can.

The next thing that factors into your score is your debt-to-credit ratio. What this means is this: you have a credit card with a limit of $5,000. If you've used $3,000 of your available credit to buy things, that means you have only $2,000 left on your card. You are using more than 50% of your available credit; this will cause your score to drop. An ideal place to be with your credit cards is to not use more than 30% at a given time. This shows lenders that you are capable of maintaining debt without going crazy and maxing out your cards. This will trigger your score to slowly rise.

The length of your credit history plays a smaller but equally important role in determining your score. The longer your history, the better. Be wary, though, if you've had a credit card for five years and take out a loan to buy a car. The length of your credit is determined by an average of all of your accounts. You may have had a card for five years, but your new auto loan will make your credit history average out to maybe 2 to 2½ years. Be mindful of this when you're thinking of opening a new line of credit.

The last factor in determining your score is going to be credit inquiries. Whenever you apply for a credit card, auto loan, or a mortgage for a house, the lender you are asking to borrow from will pull your credit reports to see if you are "trustworthy." This is considered a credit inquiry. There are two types—hard inquiries and soft inquiries. Soft inquiries have very little effect on your overall score. These are done by credit card companies to find people that may be potential customers. If you've ever received one of those "you've been preapproved" letters from a credit card company, chances are they did a soft inquiry on your credit. A hard inquiry is when you apply for something more substantial like a car loan or a mortgage. These have a higher impact on your score. A few here and there won't affect your score too badly. Too many inquiries, and lenders may be wary to approve you because they see that you've been looking for credit in a lot of places.

If you're thinking of buying a new car or house, try to apply for all of your loans at the same time. That way when they pull your credit reports, they won't see a collection of inquiries from an assortment of different creditors, thus improving your chances of getting approved.

Building Your Credit

Building good credit takes time. If you've never dealt with credit before, it can seem like a daunting task. There are some simple steps you can take to start building a healthy relationship with your credit.

A quick way to start building your credit is to get a prepaid or secured credit card from your local bank. They don't require a credit check because you're putting up your own money as collateral. Therefore, if you don't pay, you're only hurting yourself. The next thing to do is set up this card to pay something you are going to pay anyway religiously, like your phone bill. Set the card up to autopay the phone bill, then set up your bank account to autopay the credit card every month.

Once you've done this for a certain amount of time, sometimes six months to a year, your bank will notify you that they have increased your credit limit, given you your initial money back, and now you have an unsecured card. That means you've proven yourself worthy enough for a "real" credit card.

It's tempting when you get your first real credit card to go out and buy the things you feel you need. Resist this temptation! Keep paying off your phone bill with this initial card, and don't use it for anything else. Continue for another six months to a year, and you will be amazed at how much your credit score has grown since you began.

Once your score gets better, then start exploring your options as far as new cards with higher limits. Always remember, these cards aren't free money—use cards for emergencies and unexpected expenses. Even then, try to pay them off as soon as possible. Depending on the interest rate that you get, it's imperative that you pay off your cards as soon as you are able. That means paying more than the minimum payment. If all you make is the minimum payment every month, you will find yourself upside down on your credit cards. So make sure you treat credit cards with immense respect, and use them only when absolutely necessary.

Your Financial Future

It may seem strange to start thinking about retirement when you're in your mid-twenties. As professional musicians, we don't have a lot of the luxuries that come along with having a "real" job, like a 401(k) or stock options for our twilight years.

> Working as a musician, one of the things that struck me hardest
> was watching some of my mentors flail and struggle later in life
> because they hadn't planned on getting older!

You're probably not thinking right now about what your life is going to look like when you're sixty. And that's okay. I am very much a "live-in-the-moment" kind of person. It serves no purpose to worry about things that haven't happened to you yet. You have to be present in order to take advantage of the opportunities that present themselves to you.

However, it doesn't mean that you can't begin to prepare for later in life right now, just in case you're not invincible.

When I was growing up, we didn't have much in the way of money. When my grandparents decided to retire, all of a sudden there were endless trips to Toys "R" Us and Red Lobster for dinner. It was like they had won the lottery.

My grandparents came from a different generation. A generation that worked hard while they were young so they could have the freedom they always desired when they were older. Retirement was a real thing to their generation; more and more these days, people are working longer in life and retiring with much less than older generations did.

Now, there are a lot of factors that contribute to this fact, but you can do some things right now to ensure that you will be okay. And the sooner you start, the better off you will be.

IRAs

One of the easiest things you can do right now, today even, is to set up for yourself what is known as an IRA, or Individual Retirement Account. You can think of an IRA as a super-savings account.

Most savings accounts offer incentives for you to put your money into them. Perhaps, a no-fee checking account, or a higher interest rate on the money that is in the account. While a standard savings account will offer somewhere around a 1% to 2% interest rate, an IRA can offer up to a 7% interest rate. Obviously, 7% is better than 1% to 2%. IRAs can offer such a good interest rate because they have certain rules that you are required to follow.

The first thing you will need to do when you set one up is go to your local bank and ask to meet with a financial advisor. An IRA won't cost you any money to set up, but you will be asked some questions before you can get started. The first will be what is your current age. The second will be at what age (realistically) would you like to retire.

For instance, you're twenty years old and you tell the bank that you would like to retire at seventy years old, therefore in fifty years.

When you set up an IRA, you are essentially making a contract with the bank. You are telling the bank that you are twenty now, and you will contribute to this account for the next fifty years. The catch is that over the next fifty years, you can put money into this account, but you will not be able to withdraw any of it until you hit your age of retirement at seventy. For this inconvenience, the bank will give you a much better interest rate.

This may seem like a disconcerting idea: put money into an account that you don't have access to! However, an IRA has the ability to grow exponentially over the years. Because it has a high interest rate, the money in the account continuously multiplies itself by whatever the interest rate is. This is called "compound interest." This is a financial aspect that wealthy people understand. They make their money work for them, as opposed to working for their money.

Here's an example:

If you start your IRA with $1,000 and it has a 7% interest rate, after the first year, you will have $1,070 (1,000 × .07). After the second year, $1,070 gets multiplied by 7%, so after two years, it will be $1,144.90 (1070 × .07) and so on and so on.

If you let this go without putting another dime into the account, after fifty years you will end up with almost $30,000 from that initial investment of $1,000.

Crazy!

That's really good for just letting your money sit there. But you can do better.

Even though you can't take the money out of the account, you can still add money to it over the years. The more money you add, the more compound interest takes effect.

Here's another example:

You start with your initial $1,000, but you decide to add $50 every week. (If you're thinking in terms of hourly rates, $50/hour should be what you're shooting for when you work, so you are essentially setting aside an hour of your pay every week.)

Fifty dollars a week will be $200 a month = $2,400 a year.

If you started doing this at twenty and maintained it for the next fifty years, your money would balloon to over 1 million dollars.

Even crazier!!

You can do better . . .

An IRA allows you to contribute up to $5,500 a year. You just saw an example where you were putting in only $2,400, less than half of what you can actually do. Check how this one pans out.

Last example, I promise.

Putting in $5,500 a year is roughly double what was shown in the previous example. Now, change $50 a week to $100 a week (or two hours of work at $50/hour).

One hundred dollars a week will be $400 a month = $5,200 a year (not quite the maximum of $5,500, but close enough).

Once again having the discipline to do this and maintain it for the next fifty years, you would end up with roughly $2.3 million.

If you want to play around with different numbers, Bankrate.com has a really cool free calculator that you can put to use and see how much you could make with an IRA.

Two Types of IRAs

There are two types of IRAs. One is known as a traditional IRA, and the other is known as a *Roth IRA*. They both function as super-savings accounts using compound interest to balloon your savings over time.

The difference is how they work in regard to your taxes.

A traditional IRA allows you to deduct your contributions every year. If you put the full $5,500 in, you are able to write off $5,500 from your income—awesome!

The downside is when you pull the money out when you retire, you are taxed on the money you withdraw.

A Roth IRA is the opposite of a traditional. With a Roth, you aren't able to write off your contributions. However, when you retire and decide to withdraw from your account, there are zero taxes.

Both types of IRAs have their benefits. Take some time and visit your local bank. Inquire about what they can offer as far as an IRA goes. Remember, you can start an IRA with any amount of money from $1 to $100,000. You should also know that you will never be penalized for not contributing to it. You could go ten years without putting money into it, and that's fine.

If you try to withdraw the money before the retirement date that you gave the bank, you will absolutely be penalized, so much that you should just not even entertain that option.

This is a very simple step you can take right now to make sure that when you decide you want to retire, you have something that's waiting for you.

Other Options

These are just a few suggestions as to how you can prepare for your future. At some point, it may be a good idea to consult with a financial advisor to get you on the right track. Do some research, as there are many companies out there that offer these services. Don't be afraid to ask questions like "How much does each transaction cost?" "Will I have access to my money in an emergency?" "What is your commission on my account?"

A financial advisor is required to have your best interest at heart. Some are predatory, so be vigilant with whom you trust your financial future. With a little effort, you should be able to find the right person.

EPILOGUE
Parting Thoughts

Malte Mueller/Getty Images

*I*t is my hope that this book has clarified some of the most pervasive mis-conceptions about working in the music industry. I do not pretend to have all of the answers you may seek; I only have my own experiences and mistakes to share.

This road is not an easy one.

It is also not an impossible one. It requires a tremendous amount of discipline just to get your feet off the ground. And then the real work begins—the work of sustainability. If you persevere and take every opportunity as a learning experience, the reward is a (good) life of doing what you love. That's the dream, right?

Jim Carrey gave an amazing commencement speech at Maharishi University in 2014. In this speech, he tells the story of how his father could have been a great comedian but abandoned that ambition to take a "safe" job as an accountant. Carrey then talks about how his father then lost that "safe" job, and they had to do whatever was necessary just to get by. The point, Carrey says, is this: "You can fail at what you don't want, so you might as well take a chance at doing what you love."

Words to live by.

Finding Your Voice

Understand that you are unique. There is only one of you. It's easy in the arts to get sidetracked watching others' creations and feeling inadequate with our own. There is nothing to gain from this, only heartache. Others are using their unique voice to express themselves. Your job is to find and use your own.

No one in the world can do what you do. Revel in that fact.

Martha Graham, the very famous choreographer, has some insight with this:

> *"There is a vitality, a life force, an energy, a quickening that is translated through you into action, and because there is only one of you in all of time, this expression is unique. And if you block it, it will be lost. The world will not have it. It is not your business to determine how good it is nor how valuable it compares with other's expressions. It is your business to keep it yours clearly and directly, to keep the channel open. You do not even have to believe in yourself or your work. You have to keep yourself open and aware to the urges that motivate you. Keep the channel open. No artist is pleased. [There is] no satisfaction whatever at any time. There is only a queer divine dissatisfaction, a blessed unrest that keeps us marching and makes us more alive than the others."*

> —As quoted in *The Life and Work of Martha Graham* (1991) by Agnes de Mille

Find your voice and carry on. Don't become precious with your works. Create them and move on to the next.

Fear

The greatest adversary you will ever face is fear. Your fear. Fear of failure, fear of success, fear of the unknown, fear of money, fear of love.

Fear is the enemy of success. Fear can cripple even the strongest among us. How we deal with fear directly correlates to our quality of life. It's okay to be afraid. It's okay to be fearful. But if you let fear affect your decisions, you will be lost.

The answer to dealing with fear can be found in our stories. The stories of slaying dragons and going on quests into the unknown.

Joseph Campbell was a famous mythologist. He wrote a book called *The Hero with a Thousand Faces*. In the book, he connects the dots of human beings globally through storytelling. He shows that there are common themes that bind us as humans around the world through our myths and legends. Campbell shows us that "myth" is a metaphor for life.

One common theme in mythology is the slaying of monsters, dragons in particular. We must venture into the unknown. Sometimes willingly, sometimes we have it forced upon us. We must seek out the monster and destroy it. This is a metaphor for the monster that resides within us—our fear. We can let it consume us, or we can slay it and conquer our fear, our self-doubt.

This is you. You must venture into the unknown. You must slay your personal monster or be consumed by it. You must face your fear head-on. It may seem like an impossible task, but if you succeed, you will be rewarded with riches (wisdom, confidence, knowledge) beyond belief. You will evolve into something greater than you once were.

Once you are able to conquer your fear, nothing will stand in the way of your success.

Stop Worrying

One thing that is for sure in life is that nothing is for sure. It serves no purpose to worry about things you have absolutely no control over. The only thing you can control is the choices you make. You can choose to be happy or you can choose to be the victim. No one has control over your choices regardless of what you may think. As said earlier—shit happens. The choices you make in how you deal with problems that arise will affect directly how you feel.

You will make good choices and you will make bad ones. They are yours and yours alone. Yes, there are some awful people in this world that will try to take advantage of you. And sometimes they may. However, it is up to you and the choices you make to either feel sorry for yourself or to rise above it and continue on.

Do Something Else

When music becomes your job, it can be like any other job—you can burn out. You may begin to dislike it. In order to combat this, you need to do things outside of music. Find a hobby. Go on a hike. Do something else. It's important not only for your sanity but also because you need to experience other aspects of life.

Take time for yourself and find things that you enjoy. Go find the beauty that exists in the world, experience it. Then come back and create with your newfound knowledge.

Don't Forget to Breathe

The final thing I want to say to you is this . . .
BREATHE
Take a breath . . .
Even when your world is crashing down around you. Breathe.
Everything will be okay
Stay the course, make a correction if you need to. Breathe.
You messed up? Breathe.
Everything will be okay
Don't quit. Breathe.
You can do this.

Littil Swayamp

GLOSSARY

Ableton Live: Popular DAW, especially with hip-hop and EDM producers

adaptive: Adaptive music changes and evolves based on the players' choices

all-in budget: When a client has a set amount of money for an entire project

Avid Pro Tools: "Industry Standard" DAW used by most high-end production facilities

back end: Royalties or residuals earned on how well the project performs in the marketplace

backline: Gear that is rented ahead of time in the city to which you are traveling, typically, drums, amps, and keyboards

balance: Mixing term where all of the audio tracks work well with each other based on volume and EQ

broadcast ready: Term used to describe the overall perfected quality of a product, ready for commercial audio release

BITC, or burnt-in timecode: SMPTE time code "burned in" to a video file for timing and synchronization purposes

busses: Used to route multiple audio signals to a particular location within a DAW

buyout: When a company offers you a flat license fee for your music, which then allows them to use it whenever and however they want, forever

cartage: The transporting of one's equipment for either touring or studio purposes

cattle call: An audition that is open to the public

comp (n): When the best bits of all of the different takes of a performance are cut and pasted together

compound interest: The interest gained on a sum of money based on the initial principal plus the accumulated interest over a given amount of time

copyright: Grants the legal right for the creator of an original "work" of intellectual property to exclusively publish, use, and distribute it as they see fit

> Here are the US government Copyright Office forms for songs:
> https://www.copyright.gov/forms/formpa.pdf (for songs)
> https://www.copyright.gov/forms/formsr.pdf (for sound recordings)

cover band: A group that specializes in performing other artists' songs

credit inquiries: A credit check performed by a financial institution to determine one's creditworthiness

> **hard inquiries**: A credit inquiry done when looking for large financing options, such as auto loans and mortgages. These have an impact on your overall credit score.

> **soft inquiries**: A credit inquiry done when applying for smaller financing or part of a background check. Applying for a new phone plan may produce a soft inquiry. These have no impact on your credit score.

cues: Short pieces of music that once pieced together, will give you the entire scope of the score

data roaming: When your phone disconnects from its carrier's network and joins another. Common when traveling abroad and can cause large charges on your phone bill

DAW (digital audio workstation): Software programs that allow the user to record, edit, program, mix, and master music

DBA (doing business as): The operating name of a business. As an individual, you can use a pseudonym or made-up name to run your small business while it's still connected to your legal name.

debt-to-credit ratio: The amount of revolving credit you are using divided by the total amount of credit available to you

EIN, or Employment Identification Number: A unique nine-digit number assigned by the IRS to businesses

EP (extended play): An extended play recording contains more tracks than a single but fewer than a full album or long-play record.

exclusive license: No person or company other than the named licensee can use or exploit the intellectual property for a period of time.

fee-based budget: A guarantee of a specific amount of money

flat rate: Charging a fixed fee for a service, regardless of time involved

fly dates: Either one-off gigs or a short run of shows that are too far to drive to

fly rig: Everything one needs gear-wise for traveling, just made smaller so you can carry your instrument and equipment on a plane

frame rate: The measure of how quickly a number of frames appear within one second. Commonly referred to as FPS, or frames per second

game jam: A meetup of software developers where they try to create a game from scratch over the course of either a weekend or week

green room: A room set up for performers to relax when not performing

horizontal resequencing: A method of interactive composition where the music is dynamically pieced together based on a player's actions

immersion: In games, referred to as the players' mental involvement in a game

independent contractor: A self-employed person who is contracted to perform work or provide services to another entity as a nonemployee

indie (artist): Independent artist who has no funding or managerial oversight

interface (audio): Device that converts an analog signal to a digital signal for use with recording audio into a computer DAW program

IRA, or individual retirement account: A savings account with tax advantages that individuals can set up and save for long-term investments

key switches (MIDI): A MIDI note that triggers a different sample or playing technique within a sequencer

LLC, or limited liability company: A business structure that protects its owners from personal responsibility for its debts or liabilities

linear: Film music that is considered linear, meaning it goes from point A to point B and will always be the same

load-in: The time and place where a band or artist "loads" and sets up their equipment before a show

lobby call: The time everyone is meant to be up and ready to go

locked cut: The final edit of a film or other video program that a composer uses to finalize composition and timings of cues

Logic Pro: Popular DAW developed by Apple

Looping: A sound or piece that continually repeats itself over and over again

master or master recording: The complete, original recording from which all copies are made

mastering: The final step in the recording process before commercial release, when volume adjustments/balancing and audio enhancements are applied

MD (music director): Person responsible for all of the musical aspects of a show

mechanical royalty: A royalty generated whenever a song is reproduced and purchased. It's typically paid to the owner of the copyright such as the songwriter or the publisher

metadata: Digital information embedded in audio files including important data that provides additional information about the file

middleware: Software used to implement the changes in audio that happen within a game

milestone pay system: When you're paid a portion of your fee based on reaching certain milestones within the project

milestones: Significant stages of a project's development

mixing: The second to last stage in a recording's production that involves achieving balance and clarity between the instruments and vocals

mock-up: An extensive demo of a recording project built using virtual software/hardware instruments used as a stand-in for acoustic instruments

nonexclusive license: Grants the licensee rights to use an intellectual property but also allows the licensor the right to continue exploiting the intellectual property to be licensed

per diem ("per day"): Daily allowance paid to performers while on tour

person of contact (POC): Person responsible for coordinating entertainers at an event. Usually designated in the entertainer's contract

pitch: A presentation of an idea or piece of music for consideration to be used in a particular project

plug-ins: Computer software that adds new functions to a host program without altering the host program itself (e.g., software instruments, EQs, compressors)

points: One percent (1%) of every dollar the project earns in sales

prepaid or secured credit card: A type of credit card that is backed by a cash deposit from the cardholder

producer (music): Person responsible for bringing to fruition the ideas and vision of a client or artist

recalls: Reopening a mixed project for additional tweaks and adjustments

reference mix: A reference recording that captures the overall sound a client or artist has in mind

revisions: Reopening a project to enact a set of changes that corrects or improves the recording

Roth IRA: A type of individual retirement account where annual contributions are not tax deductible. However, once the account matures, the account holder pays no tax on withdrawal of funds.

rough cuts: Unfinished edits of a film or video project, used to give the composer a sense of feel and timing for a project

royalty: A sum of money paid to the owner of a work for the purchase, usage, or public performance of their work

sample rate: The resolution of an audio file based on the number of samples that occur per second (e.g., 48 kHz = 48,000 samples per second). The general rule is, the higher the sample rate, the higher the resolution of the audio. However, higher sample rates create larger files. Industry standard for audio is 44.1 kHz, and video standard is 48 kHz.

sends/returns/effects: Bussing that allows the sending of multiple sounds through the same effects, such as reverbs or delays

showrunner: Person responsible for the overall creative and management decisions within a television program

side-person: A musician who supports or "backs up" another artist

signal flow: The path audio takes from its source to its output

SoundCloud: Online audio distribution platform and music sharing website

splits: Percentages of ownership for a song or composition with multiple writers

spotting session: Where the composer and either the director or producers of the project watch a "cut" of the film and decide where the music should or shouldn't be placed

statute of limitations: A law that sets the maximum amount of time that parties involved in a dispute have to initiate legal proceedings

stems (short for "stereo masters"): Files from a recording separated by instrument or group of instruments, often for the purpose of creating an alternate mix

subbing: Filling in for a regular musician when they are not available

sync fee: Payment made to the songwriter or music publisher to use a song in synchronization with visual images onscreen

tags: Metadata that allows a file to be searchable in a database

time code: SMPTE time code is an electronic signal that is used to identify a precise location on time-based media, such as audio or video tape or in digital systems.

tour wranglers: Persons responsible for the finding and hiring of musicians for touring purposes

trigger: A sound used in video games to signify an event (e.g., a door opening or finding a treasure)

vertical layering: In video games, when you start with an initial loop and as the player interacts and moves around the environment of the game, other loops come in and out, creating different layers of intensity

waveform: A graphical representation of how sound moves through the air

woodshed (v): To practice

work-for-hire: One hired to provide a service but is not affiliated or employed by the one who hires them

write-off: A deduction from the value of earnings by the amount of an expense or loss

RECOMMENDED READING

Borg, Bobby.
　Music Marketing for the DIY Musician: Creating and Executing a Plan of Attack on a Low Budget (Music Pro Guides). Lanham, MD: Rowman & Littlefield, 2020.

Borg, Bobby, and Michael Eames.
　Introduction to Music Publishing for Musicians: Business and Creative Perspectives for the New Music Industry. Lanham, MD: Rowman & Littlefield, 2021.

Brabec, Jeffrey, and Todd Brabec.
　Music, Money and Success: The Insider's Guide to Making Money in the Music Business. Eighth edition. New York, NY: Omnibus Press, Schirmer Trade Books, 2018.

Campbell, Joseph.
　The Hero with a Thousand Faces. Third edition. San Francisco, CA: New World Library, 2008.

Copyright Registration of Musical Compositions and Sound Recording.
　Circular 56A. Revised. Washington, DC: United States Copyright Office, 2021.

RECOMMENDED READING

Hill, Napoleon.
Think and Grow Rich. Revised and enlarged edition. Los Angeles, CA: TarcherPerigee, 2005.

Marino, Tracey, and Vance Marino.
Hey! That's My Song! A Guide to Getting Music Placements in Film, TV, and Media. Edited by Ronny Schiff. Guilford, CT: Backbeat Books, 2022.

Musashi, Miyamoto.
The Book of Five Rings. Translated by Thomas Cleary. Boulder, CO: Shambhala Library, 2005.

Passman, Donald S.
All You Need to Know about the Music Business. Tenth Edition. New York, NY: Simon & Schuster, 2019.

Pressfield, Steven.
The War of Art. New York, NY/Los Angeles, CA: Black Irish Entertainment LLC, 2002.

Rona, Jeff.
The Reel World: Scoring for Pictures. Third Edition. Edited by Ronny Schiff. Lanham, MD: Rowman & Littlefield, 2022.

Winogradsky, Steve.
Music Publishing: The Complete Guide. Second Edition. Edited by David Lowery. Van Nuys, CA: Alfred Publishing Company, 2019.

INDEX

ABOUT THE AUTHOR

Kris Hawkins
Littil Swayamp

Kris has made it his mission to educate and prepare aspiring musicians for the challenges that they will face once they enter the industry.

Kris Hawkins is an Emmy-winning music producer, studio guitarist, and award-winning educator living in Los Angeles.

Kris began his professional career as a guitarist twenty-five years ago in Florida, eventually making the move to Los Angeles in the early 2000s. Upon arrival, he immediately became an in-demand session musician for the likes of Enrique Iglesias, Christina Aguilera, Dr. Dre, Dr. Luke, Cathy Dennis, and many more.

After his successful tenure as a session musician, Kris shifted his focus to the production side of music, finding, developing, and pitching songs and artists for labels such as Sony, Universal Music Group, Hollywood Records, and a slew of independents.

Kris has also created an extensive catalog of music for use in film, television, and advertising. He's secured placements with Bud Light, History Channel, Discovery Channel, National Geographic Channel, and more.

In 2014, Kris accepted a position at the prestigious Musicians Institute College of Contemporary Music in Hollywood, California, where he developed curriculum to help young musicians navigate the perils of being a professional musician. Having endured the hard lessons of the music industry firsthand, he made it his mission to educate and prepare aspiring musicians on the challenges that they will face once they enter the industry. He's been awarded the "Faculty of the Year" award for his division three times.

Kris splits his time these days composing music for film, TV, and video games at his home studio in Los Angeles; performing live shows; doing session work; and teaching at the Musicians Institute College of Contemporary Music.

The Business of Being a Musician
Creating a Lasting and Sustainable Career as a Professional Musician

A Handbook
By Kris Hawkins

Edited by Ronny S. Schiff

Kris in producing mode . . .
Kris's camera

CPSIA information can be obtained
at www.ICGtesting.com
Printed in the USA
LVHW111155110822
725646LV00003B/374